Contents

Make-Ahead Magic

"Make ahead"—to a busy cook, these words may sound like a magic incantation. But there's really no magic involved, just down-to-earth planning. Many recipes even adapt well to advance preparation. In sauces, soups, and stews, for example, the flavor often improves after a waiting period between cooking and serving.

For today's cook, the advantages of a make-ahead approach are easy to understand. They include appetizers that free you from the kitchen to mingle with guests; soups that let you sit down sooner; main courses ready after long workdays or when unexpected company arrives; salads and vegetables that demand no last-minute fuss; and breads and desserts that pamper you with their freshness. You can pick one course to help simplify your life—or create a complete meal in advance.

Whether you're planning a party or coping with a hurried week, this book can guide you to delicious success. In addition to menu suggestions, we include special features on salad dressings, salsas, beverages, and even breakfasts to create now and serve later.

The secret to the make-ahead art is a careful strategy. After you've selected your recipes, write a comprehensive shopping list; then purchase all of the ingredients. For best-tasting results, start with the freshest ingredients you can find.

The U.S.D.A. Food Safety and Inspection Service cautions against letting prepared food stand at room temperature for more than 2 hours. For safety's sake, follow the storage instructions given for each recipe and keep perishable food, such as casseroles, hot or cold as required—not in between.

When you're ready to serve a make-ahead dish, treat it as you would any other food. With an eye to presentation, choose attractive serving pieces—such as a decorative platter, gleaming silverware, or a favorite tablecloth. Or dress up a make-ahead meal with garnishes of citrus peel, herbs, or sculpted vegetables.

To prepare this book, the standard for including a recipe was that it could be made at least 1 day, or 24 hours, before serving. Many recipes can be made further in advance. To get an even longer head start, consider freezing certain dishes (see "Frozen Assets" on the following page).

For delicious food to appear, disappear, and then reappear may sound like sleight of hand. But you won't need a top hat and wand: it's easy to make magic on your own with make-ahead cooking.

A Word About Our Nutritional Data

For our recipes, we provide a nutritional analysis stating calorie count; grams of protein, carbohydrates, and total fat; and milligrams of cholesterol and sodium. Generally, the nutritional information applies to a single serving, based on the largest number of servings given for each recipe.

The nutritional analysis does not include optional ingredients or those for which no specific amount is stated. If an ingredient is listed with an option, the information was calculated using the first choice. Likewise, if a range is given for the amount of an ingredient, values were figured based on the first, lower amount.

Make-Ahead
COOK BOOK

By the Editors of Sunset Books and Sunset Magazine

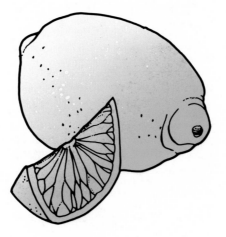

Lane Publishing Co. ■ **Menlo Park, California**

Elegance is easy when your menu features make-ahead Broccoli- & Cheese-stuffed Chicken Breasts (recipe on page 40).

Research & Text
Sue Brownlee

Contributing Editor
Susan Warton

Coordinating Editor
Linda J. Selden

Design
Joe di Chiarro

Illustrations
Rik Olson

Photography
Tom Wyatt

Photo Stylist
JoAnn Masaoka Van Atta

Food Stylist
Elizabeth Gamburd

Help for the Busy Cook

When you enjoy cooking creatively, yet your time is limited, adapting recipes to your busy schedule can be just the answer you need. This book does the rescheduling for you. All the recipes, from elegant appetizers to glorious desserts, can be prepared at least a day ahead. You then store the food and present it when you're ready—all with a minimum of last-minute fuss.

Lunch, dinner, and even breakfast ideas are here, as well as make-ahead menus for all kinds of parties. Discover classic entrées and new culinary adventures, salads and sauces, all of which can wait for your convenience. You'll also find valuable information on freezing food so you can extend storage times even longer.

We extend special thanks to Dr. George K. York, Cooperative Extension Food Technologist, University of California at Davis, and Kathryn J. Boor, Research Associate Food Science Extension, University of California at Davis, for reviewing our recipes and giving technical advice on food storage.

We also wish to thank Sally James for her assistance in the kitchen, and to Fran Feldman for carefully editing the manuscript. We extend our appreciation to Abacus Home Accessories, The Best of All Worlds, Crate & Barrel, and Menlo Park Hardware for their generosity in sharing props for use in our photographs.

For our recipes, we provide a nutritional analysis (please see page 4) prepared by Hill Nutrition Associates, Inc., of New York.

About the Recipes

All of the recipes in this book were tested and developed in the *Sunset* test kitchens.

Food and Entertaining Editor, Sunset Magazine: **Jerry Anne Di Vecchio.**

Cover: Treat family or guests to this handsome dinner of Pork Loin Stuffed with Two Cheeses (recipe on page 35), Minty Carrots & Wild Rice (recipe on page 65), Glazed Roasted Onions (recipe on page 67), and Corn & Red Pepper Relish Salad (recipe on page 60). Like magic, all the recipes can be made ahead. Design by Williams & Ziller. Photography by Tom Wyatt. Photo styling by Allyson Anthony. Food styling by Elizabeth Gamburd.

Editor, Sunset Books: Elizabeth L. Hogan

First printing April 1989

Frozen Assets

Freezing is a convenience that's much appreciated in make-ahead cooking. Freezing prepared food significantly extends its storage time, granting you even more freedom from last-minute fuss. But for the best results, it's important to follow certain guidelines.

The shorter the time food is frozen and the colder the temperature of the freezer, the higher the quality of the food. When food is stored at 0°F or less, food spoilage organisms become inactive: they neither grow nor multiply. If a food product suitable for freezing is properly packaged and stored at 0°F or less for no longer than its recommended storage time, it can retain much of its original quality, flavor, and texture.

The principles of freezing. As food freezes, the water it contains expands and forms ice crystals, which can push and puncture food cell walls; as the food thaws, natural juices escape through the walls, altering to various degrees the food's texture and flavor.

The larger the ice crystal, the greater the cell wall damage and loss of liquid. When freezing is fast, smaller crystals form. Thus, foods frozen quickly have the best quality after thawing. And to freeze fast, the food must be cool.

Wrapping and freezing. The freezer dries out improperly wrapped food, causing the changes in color, texture, and flavor sometimes called freezer burn.

To protect food from dehydration, seal it in a moisture- and vapor-resistant material—for example, heavy freezer paper, plastic freezer wrap, freezer bags, or aluminum foil. Be sure to press out all the air. Rigid containers of glass, metal, or plastic also work, but remember to leave sufficient space under the lids to allow for expansion of any liquid.

Using freezer tape, label the package with the recipe name or type of food and the date stored.

Place the food in the coldest part of the freezer near the coils or cold air outlet, leaving space for air to circulate. (Freeze no more than 2 to 3 pounds of food at a time for each cubic foot of freezer space; otherwise, the freezer may not work efficiently and freezing will be slowed.)

Thawing food. When food is held at temperatures between 40° and 140°F, bacteria can multiply rapidly. Higher temperatures destroy most bacteria; lower temperatures retard their growth.

The safest way to thaw meat, poultry, and fish is to remove the food from the freezer and defrost it in the refrigerator. For faster thawing you can put the frozen food into a waterproof container and run cold water over it; or place the container in cold water and change the water often.

Thawed combination dishes, such as casseroles, stews, and meat dishes, should be refrigerated (but not for more than 24 hours) until you're ready to heat and serve them. Certain foods, such as fruit and some baked goods, can safely be thawed at room temperature. Microwave ovens thaw food quickly and well; follow the manufacturer's directions for defrosting.

What to freeze: Many of the dishes in this book can be successfully frozen (see specific recipes for recommendations). For optimum quality, freezer temperature must be 0°F or below; use a freezer thermometer to check temperature. Emulsions, like mayonnaise and hollandaise, and foods with a cream sauce are not good freezer candidates. Cooked meats, poultry, and fish hold up best when frozen in a sauce.

Recipes that rely on potatoes, hard-cooked egg whites, cooked noodles, rice, or fried tortillas can change texture when frozen. Likewise, changes in texture can occur with foods in cream sauces or emulsions (mayonnaise and hollandaise, for example). Seasonings are also affected by freezing: spiced foods may taste quite different after being frozen. For these reasons, we do not recommend freezing these types of dishes.

Make-Ahead Menus

No matter what the occasion—elegant dinner party or relaxed family get-together—you can be prepared completely in advance. Here are suggestions for appetizers through desserts that can give you a head start on any kind of celebration.

Planning a party? Make it memorable by serving Brazilian Feijoada with Farofa (recipe on page 29), a complete feast that includes meats, black beans, brown rice, and salsa. Prepare most of it, along with a dessert of Brazilian Coconut Custard (recipe on page 88), well ahead of time; then relax and join the fiesta.

Appetizers

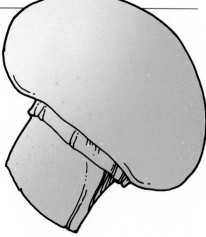

To welcome a guest, to create a mood, even to make a light meal—appetizers are the answer. The tempting mouthfuls in this chapter will delight everyone, including the cook, because they demand little, if any, last-minute preparation. For any occasion, Spicy Country Pâté and mustardy Marinated Mushrooms with Tarragon are ready when you are. Golden Polenta Diamonds add the rich taste of Gorgonzola cheese to an Italian dinner, while Baked Lumpia Rolls, plump with water chestnuts and bamboo shoots, introduce an Asian menu. Before a cool springtime supper, offer Asparagus with Toasted Sesame Mayonnaise. Or warm up a winter evening with spicy Chinese Crab Claws.

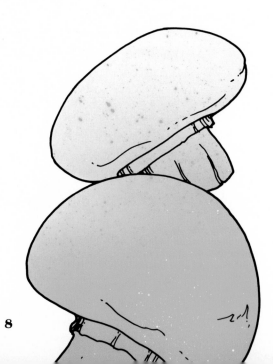

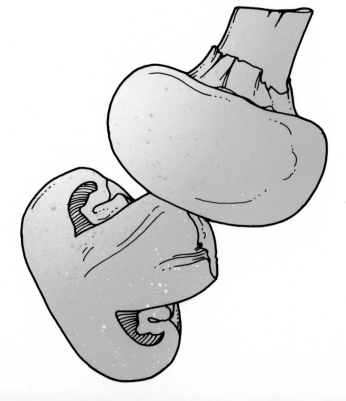

Asparagus with Toasted Sesame Mayonnaise

Initial preparation: About 15 minutes
Storage time: Asparagus: 1 day; mayonnaise: 2 days
Final preparation: None

Per serving asparagus: 11 calories, 1 g protein, 2 g carbohydrates, .10 g total fat, 0 mg cholesterol, .96 mg sodium

Per teaspoon mayonnaise: 89 calories, .41 g protein, .57 g carbohydrates, 10 g total fat, 11 mg cholesterol, 46 mg sodium

Take advantage of spring's vivid green asparagus with this elegant, yet informal appetizer. Both the asparagus and the savory mayonnaise can be prepared in advance, leaving plenty of time to arrange vases of spring blooms.

Toasted Sesame Mayonnaise (recipe follows)
2 pounds asparagus

Make-ahead steps: Prepare Toasted Sesame Mayonnaise.

Snap off and discard tough ends of asparagus. Peel stalks, if desired. Plunge into cold water to clean; lift out and drain.

Pour water to a depth of 1 inch into a 12- to 14-inch frying pan and bring to a boil over high heat. Add asparagus, reduce heat, and simmer, uncovered, until barely tender when pierced (3 to 4 minutes). Drain and immerse in ice water until cold; drain again. Cover and refrigerate for up to 1 day.

To serve: Offer asparagus with mayonnaise for dipping. Makes 8 to 10 servings.

Toasted Sesame Mayonnaise. In a 6- to 8-inch frying pan, combine 2 tablespoons **sesame seeds** with ¼ cup **salad oil** over medium-low heat. Cook, stirring, until seeds are golden (3 to 5 minutes). Stir in ¾ cup more salad oil; let mixture cool.

In a blender, combine 1 large **egg,** 1 clove **garlic,** 2 tablespoons **white wine vinegar,** and 1 teaspoon **honey;** whirl until smooth. With motor running, slowly add oil mixture in a thin, steady stream. Blend in 1 tablespoon **soy sauce.** Season to taste with **salt.** Cover and refrigerate for up to 2 days.

Golden Polenta Diamonds

Initial preparation: About 45 minutes
Storage time: 2 days in refrigerator; 2 months in freezer
Final preparation: About 1 hour and 5 minutes

Per serving: 70 calories, 3 g protein, 7 g carbohydrates, 3 g total fat, 8 mg cholesterol, 298 mg sodium

Two classic Italian ingredients, polenta and Gorgonzola cheese, pair up in this easy appetizer. Delicious hot or at room temperature, the bite-size diamonds can be made with regular cornmeal if you can't find coarse-ground polenta.

2 tablespoons butter or margarine
1 medium-size onion, finely chopped
5½ cups regular-strength chicken broth
1¾ cups polenta (Italian-style cornmeal) or yellow cornmeal
½ to ¾ pound Gorgonzola cheese

Make-ahead steps: In a 4- to 5-quart pan, melt butter over medium-high heat. Add onion and cook, stirring, until onion begins to brown (about 7 minutes). Add 4 cups of the broth; cover and bring to a boil over high heat.

Mix polenta with remaining 1½ cups broth. Add polenta mixture to broth. Cook, stirring, until thickened. Reduce heat to low; continue to cook, stirring, until polenta is stiff enough to stop flowing about 10 seconds after a spoon is drawn across bottom of pan (15 to 20 minutes). Immediately pour into a buttered 10- by 15-inch baking pan.

Cut cheese into ¼-inch-thick slices. Place on polenta in parallel rows about 1 inch apart, pressing cheese partway into polenta. Cool, cut through polenta between bands of cheese to make rows about 1 inch wide. Then cut diagonally across rows at 1-inch intervals. Cover and refrigerate for up to 2 days. (Or freeze for up to 2 months. Thaw overnight in refrigerator; or defrost in a microwave following manufacturer's directions.)

To serve: Bring to room temperature. Broil until cheese is sizzling (about 5 minutes). Serve hot or at room temperature. Makes about 30 servings.

Need a no-fuss appetizer? Relax—here it is. Both the crisp toast
triangles and creamy Dried Tomato Torta (recipe on facing page) can be
made well ahead of the party.

Marinated Mushrooms with Tarragon

Initial preparation: About 15 minutes
Storage time: 4 days
Final preparation: None

Per serving: 113 calories, 2 g protein, 7 g carbohydrates, 9 g total fat, 0 mg cholesterol, 4 mg sodium

Try this for a perfect party opener: sauté small whole mushrooms with thinly sliced onion; then mix the vegetables with a mustardy marinade flavored with fresh tarragon.

1½ pounds small mushrooms
⅓ cup salad oil
1 medium-size onion, thinly sliced
⅔ cup red wine vinegar
2 teaspoons firmly packed brown sugar
2 teaspoons minced fresh tarragon leaves or ¾ teaspoon dry tarragon
1 teaspoon dry mustard
Salt

Make-ahead steps: In a 4- to 5-quart pan, combine mushrooms with 1 tablespoon of the oil over medium-high heat. Cook, stirring, until mushrooms are lightly browned (about 5 minutes). Add onion and cook until slightly soft (about 5 minutes). Spoon vegetables into a bowl; set aside.

To pan add vinegar, brown sugar, tarragon, mustard, and remaining oil. Cook until mixture is hot (about 1 minute); pour over mushroom mixture. Season to taste with salt. Let cool; cover and refrigerate for up to 4 days. Makes 6 to 8 servings.

Pictured on facing page

Dried Tomato Torta

Initial preparation: About 15 minutes, plus about 20 minutes for chilling
Storage time: 3 days
Final preparation: Garnish

Per serving: 452 calories, 11 g protein, 27 g carbohydrates, 34 g total fat, 84 mg cholesterol, 775 mg sodium

Dried tomatoes add dramatic flavor, color, and texture to this rich appetizer. You can make the cheese torta and accompanying toast triangles several days ahead. At the last minute, add fresh basil leaves for extra elegance.

Toast Triangles (directions follow)
1 cup (½ lb.) each cream cheese and unsalted butter, softened
1 cup (about 5 oz.) grated Parmesan cheese
½ cup dried tomatoes packed in oil, drained (reserve oil)
About 2 cups fresh basil leaves, lightly packed

Make-ahead steps: Prepare Toast Triangles.

In an electric mixer or food processor, beat cream cheese, butter, and Parmesan cheese until very smoothly blended.

Cut 4 of the tomatoes into thin strips; set aside. In a blender, combine remaining tomatoes, oil, and about ½ cup of the cheese mixture; whirl until tomatoes are very smoothly puréed. Pour purée back into bowl with cheese mixture and beat to blend. Cover and refrigerate until firm enough to shape (about 20 minutes).

Mound cheese on a platter. Cover with an inverted bowl and refrigerate for up to 3 days.

To serve: Bring to room temperature. Arrange basil leaves and reserved tomato strips around torta; serve with toast. For individual servings, spread cheese on toast; top with a basil leaf and a tomato strip. Makes 8 to 10 servings.

Toast Triangles. Split 6 rounds of 6-inch **pocket breads** in half. Cut each round into 6 triangles. Place in a single layer in two 10- by 15-inch baking pans. Bake in a 400° oven for 3 minutes. Switch pan positions and continue baking until lightly toasted (about 2 more minutes). Let cool. Wrap airtight and store at room temperature for up to 3 days. Makes 72 triangles.

Speedy Starters

Appetizers that take little time to prepare are a hit with any hostess. Most of the ones here take less than half an hour and can be made well in advance.

Salmon Pâté

½ pound boned and skinned smoked salmon or trout
½ cup (¼ lb.) butter or margarine
1 tablespoon *each* minced shallots and Dijon mustard
¼ teaspoon fresh thyme or ⅛ teaspoon dry thyme leaves

Make-ahead steps: In a food processor or blender, combine salmon, butter, shallots, mustard, and thyme; whirl until smooth. Spoon into a small crock; cover and refrigerate for up to 3 days. (Or freeze for up to 6 months. Thaw overnight in refrigerator; or defrost in a microwave following manufacturer's directions.) Makes 1½ cups. Serve with toast.

Per tablespoon: 46 calories, 2 g protein, .15 g carbohydrates, 4 g total fat, 13 mg cholesterol, 132 mg sodium

Eggplant & Goat Cheese Rolls

7 Oriental eggplants (about 1 lb. *total*) or 1 regular globe eggplant (about 1 lb.), stemmed
1½ tablespoons olive oil
3 ounces soft goat cheese, such as Montrachet
⅓ cup packed watercress sprigs, washed and crisped

Make-ahead steps: Cut eggplants lengthwise into ¼- to ⅓-inch-thick slices. Place in a single layer in two 10- by 15-inch rimmed baking pans. Lightly brush both sides of eggplants with oil.

Bake, uncovered, in a 450° oven for 8 minutes. Turn and continue baking until very soft when pressed (about 5 more minutes). Remove from oven and let cool.

Place about ½ teaspoon of the cheese at 1 end of each slice. Top with equal portions of watercress; let leaves hang over edges. Roll up. Cover and refrigerate for up to 1 day. Makes 20 to 24 rolls, 5 or 6 appetizer servings.

Per serving: 101 calories, 4 g protein, 6 g carbohydrates, 8 g total fat, 13 mg cholesterol, 92 mg sodium

Quail Eggs with Toasted Pepper

1½ dozen quail eggs
2 teaspoons salt
2 tablespoons cracked pepper

Make-ahead steps: In a 1½- to 2-quart pan, cover quail eggs with water and bring to a boil over high heat. Reduce heat and simmer, uncovered, for 6 minutes. Run cold water over eggs and drain; refrigerate for up to 3 days.

In a small frying pan, combine salt and pepper over medium heat. Cook, shaking pan often, until salt is pale gold (about 5 minutes). Spoon into a small bowl. Cover and let stand for up to 1 week. Serve as a dip for peeled eggs. Makes 6 servings.

Per serving: 48 calories, 4 g protein, 1 g carbohydrates, 3 g total fat, 228 mg cholesterol, 734 mg sodium

Lime & Chili Vegetables

24 radishes
1 pound jicama, peeled
3 tablespoons *each* lime juice and tequila, or all lime juice
2 tablespoons chili powder
1 teaspoon salt

Make-ahead steps: Remove all but a few of best-looking leaves from radishes; rinse. Cut jicama lengthwise into ½-inch-thick sticks. Place vegetables in a dish. Cover and refrigerate for up to 1 day.

To serve: Mix lime juice and tequila. In another bowl, mix chili powder and salt. Serve with vegetables. Makes about 8 servings.

Per serving: 44 calories, 1 g protein, 6 g carbohydrates, .49 g total fat, 0 mg cholesterol, 301 mg sodium

Beef & Broccoli

⅔ pound cooked boneless roast beef or turkey breast
3 cups broccoli flowerets
2 small packages (3 oz. *each*) cream cheese
¼ cup prepared horseradish
⅓ cup plain yogurt
1 teaspoon cracked pepper
Salt

Make-ahead steps: Cut meat into ½-inch cubes. Arrange on a platter with broccoli. Beat cream cheese, horseradish, yogurt, and pepper until smooth. Salt to taste. Cover and refrigerate beef platter and dip separately for up to 1 day. Makes 6 servings.

Per serving: 229 calories, 20 g protein, 6 g carbohydrates, 14 g total fat, 73 mg cholesterol, 151 mg sodium

Spicy Country Pâté

Initial preparation: About 1¾ hours
Storage time: 3 days in refrigerator; 6 months in freezer
Final preparation: None

Per serving: 111 calories, 9 g protein, 4 g carbohydrates, 6 g total fat, 170 mg cholesterol, 307 mg sodium

Serve this herb-spiced loaf on baguette slices with Dijon mustard.

- 1 **pound** *each* **chicken livers and bulk pork sausage**
- 2 **large eggs**
- ¼ **teaspoon ground cinnamon**
- 1 **teaspoon** *each* **ground pepper and dry thyme leaves**
- ½ **cup fine dry bread crumbs**
- 1 **tablespoon** *each* **lemon juice and Worcestershire**
- 1 **small onion, minced**
- 3 **cloves garlic, minced or pressed**
- 2 **tablespoons minced parsley**
- ½ **teaspoon salt**
- 3 **bay leaves**

Make-ahead steps: In a food processor or a food chopper fitted with a fine blade, combine livers and sausage; grind until fine. Place in a bowl; mix in eggs, cinnamon, pepper, thyme, bread crumbs, lemon juice, Worcestershire, onion, garlic, parsley, and salt.

Press mixture into a 6-cup terrine or a 4½- by 8½-inch loaf pan; press bay leaves on top. Bake, uncovered, in a 350° oven until firm to touch (about 1½ hours). Pour off and discard fat. Let cool; cover and refrigerate for up to 3 days. (Or freeze for up to 6 months. Thaw overnight in refrigerator; or defrost in a microwave following manufacturer's directions.) Makes 12 to 16 servings.

Baked Lumpia Rolls

Initial preparation: About 1¼ hours
Storage time: 3 days in refrigerator; 6 months in freezer
Final preparation time: About 15 minutes

Per lumpia roll: 130 calories, 8 g protein, 18 g carbohydrates, 3 g total fat, 34 mg cholesterol, 162 mg sodium

Per teaspoon sauce: 27 calories, .02 g protein, 7 g carbohydrates, 0 g total fat, 0 mg cholesterol, 34 mg sodium

Crisp, savory *lumpia* is the Philippines' eggroll. It's also the name of the wrapper used (or substitute spring roll or egg roll wrappers).

- ¾ **pound lean ground pork**
- 1 **medium-size carrot, peeled and minced**
- 1 **medium-size onion, chopped**
- 1 **can (8 oz.) water chestnuts, drained and chopped**
- 1 **can (8 oz.) bamboo shoots, drained and minced**
- 8 **cloves garlic, minced or pressed**
- 2 **tablespoons soy sauce**
- 1 **teaspoon pepper**
  About 30 lumpia wrappers (about 10-inch diameter), spring roll wrappers (about 8 inches square), or egg roll wrappers (about 6 inches square)
- 1 **large egg, beaten**
  Dipping Sauce (recipe follows)

Make-ahead steps: In a large bowl, combine pork, carrot, onion, water chestnuts, bamboo shoots, garlic, soy sauce, and pepper. Stir until thoroughly combined.

To assemble each appetizer, mound 2 tablespoons of the filling 2 inches in from 1 edge of wrapper, leaving a ¾-inch margin on each end. Fold flap over filling; tuck under to secure. Roll over once; then fold in ends. Brush open edge of wrapper with beaten egg. Continue rolling. Place rolls, seam sides down, slightly apart in 10- by 15-inch baking pans covered with plastic wrap.

Bake rolls, uncovered, in a 450° oven, turning once or twice with a wide spatula, until golden brown (about 20 minutes). For even browning, switch pan positions halfway through baking. Let cool; cover and refrigerate for up to 3 days. (Or freeze for up to 6 months. Thaw overnight in refrigerator; or defrost in a microwave following manufacturer's directions.)

To serve: Reheat, uncovered, in a 450° oven until hot (about 10 minutes), turning rolls to keep color even. Meanwhile, prepare Dipping Sauce and offer with hot lumpia. Makes about 60 pieces, about 15 servings.

Dipping Sauce. In a 2- to 3-quart pan, combine 1 cup firmly packed **brown sugar,** ½ cup **white vinegar,** and 1 tablespoon **soy sauce** over high heat. Cook, stirring, until sugar dissolves. Mix 1 teaspoon **cornstarch** with 2 tablespoons **water;** add to sugar mixture and cook, stirring, until sauce boils. Remove from heat and add 2 tablespoons minced **fresh ginger.**

Pictured on facing page

Elegant Scandinavian Gravlax

Initial preparation: About 15 minutes, plus at least 1 day for chilling
Storage time: 2 to 3 days in refrigerator; 2 months in freezer
Final preparation: Garnish

Per serving: 128 calories, 14 g protein, 7 g carbohydrates, 5 g total fat, 39 mg cholesterol, 1,681 mg sodium

Salt, sugar, and fresh dill transform fresh salmon into Scandinavia's elegant delicacy *gravlax.* You can cure the fish up to 4 days before enjoying the paper-thin slices with sour cream, lemon, chives, and rye bread.

¼ **cup salt**
½ **cup firmly packed brown sugar**
2 **teaspoons fennel seeds, crushed**
1 **teaspoon black peppercorns, crushed**
⅓ **cup chopped fresh dill**
2½- to 3-pound salmon fillet
Sour cream
Lemon wedges
Thinly sliced chives
Rye bread

Make-ahead steps: Mix salt, sugar, fennel seeds, pepper, and dill. Rub mixture into both sides of fish. Place, skin side up, in a 12- by 17-inch roasting pan. Cover; place a heavy pan (containing a 4- or 5-lb. can) on top. Refrigerate for 1 to 2 days, basting occasionally. Pat fish dry. Wrap tightly and refrigerate for up to 2 more days. (Or freeze for up to 2 months. Thaw overnight in refrigerator, or defrost in a microwave following manufacturer's directions.)

To serve: Place fish, skin side down, on a platter and thinly slice across grain. Serve with sour cream, lemon, chives, and rye bread. Makes 12 to 16 servings.

Chinese Crab Claws

Initial preparation: About 45 minutes
Storage time: 1 day in refrigerator; 1 month in freezer
Final preparation: About 5 to 10 minutes

Per serving crab: 100 calories, 12 g protein, 1 g carbohydrates, 5 g total fat, 48 mg cholesterol, 134 mg sodium

Per teaspoon sauce: 3 calories, .18 g protein, .55 g carbohydrates, 0 g total fat, 0 mg cholesterol, 193 mg sodium

This convenient appetizer comes with its own handle. First, coat the meat portion of cooked crab claws with a paste of seasoned sole and more crab. Brown the claws in hot oil. To serve, bake; guests dip the hot claws—holding the pincers—into a lime and chile sauce.

1 **large egg white**
¼ **cup sliced green onions (including tops)**
1 **tablespoon *each* dry sherry and minced fresh ginger**
2 **teaspoons cornstarch**
¼ **teaspoon *each* pepper and sesame oil**
¼ **pound sole fillets**
¼ **pound crabmeat**
12 **to 14 (about 1 lb. *total*) cooked crab claws, including pincers, with part of the shell sawed off; thaw if frozen**
Salad oil
Lime Sauce (recipe follows)

Make-ahead steps: In a food processor or blender, combine egg white, green onions, sherry, ginger, cornstarch, pepper, sesame oil, and sole; whirl until smoothly puréed. Pour into a bowl and mix in crabmeat. Spread purée evenly over meat in each claw. Place coated claws on wax paper.

Pour oil to a depth of 1½ inches into a deep 2- to 3-quart pan and heat to 350°F on a deep-frying thermometer. When oil is hot, add claws, 3 at a time, and cook, uncovered, until coating is golden brown (3 to 4 minutes). As claws are cooked, lift out with a slotted spoon and drain on paper towels. Let cool; arrange in a single layer in a 10- by 15-inch baking pan. Cover and refrigerate for up to 1 day. (Or freeze for up to 1 month. Thaw overnight in refrigerator, or defrost in a microwave following manufacturer's directions.)

To serve: Bake claws, uncovered, in a 275° oven until hot (5 to 10 minutes). Meanwhile, prepare Lime Sauce and offer with claws. Makes 4 to 7 servings, 2 to 3 claws each.

Lime Sauce. Mix 3 tablespoons *each* **soy sauce** and **lime juice** with 1 **fresh small hot green chile** (such as jalapeño or serrano), stemmed, seeded, and chopped.

On the next special occasion, treat your guests to Elegant Scandinavian Gravlax (recipe on facing page). Fresh salmon is cured, flavored with dill and fennel, and served with plenty of sour cream, lemon, and chives.

Soups

Either hot or cold, as a first course or finale, filled with meat or vegetables, soups satisfy as few other dishes can. They also adapt readily to make-ahead cooking. The soup selections of this chapter run the gamut from hearty, ham-filled Split Pea to a delicate purée of vegetables in Golden Garden Soup. For color and drama, choose between Grilled Corn Soup with chile and cilantro creams and simple Red Onion Borscht. You can either warm up or cool off with Carrot Yogurt Soup—it's wonderful hot or cold. And, for fruit fanciers, we offer spicy Hot Ginger Pear Soup.

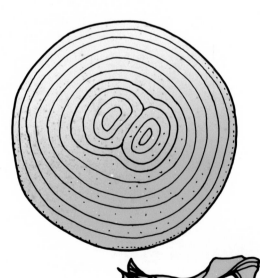

Split Pea Soup

Initial preparation: About 3¼ hours
Storage time: 5 days in refrigerator; 12 months in freezer
Final preparation: About 20 minutes

Per serving: 210 calories, 15 g protein, 31 g carbohydrates, 3 g total fat, 12 mg cholesterol, 960 mg sodium

When the fog outside is as thick as split pea soup, fortify the family indoors with the same thing. Our Swedish soup needs little attention and can be made up to 5 days ahead. Serve with dollops of robust German-style mustard.

- 1½ **pounds (3 cups) dry yellow split peas**
- **About 3 quarts water**
- 2 **large onions, chopped**
- 3 **large carrots, peeled and chopped**
- 1½ **teaspoons dry marjoram**
- 3 **to 4 pounds smoked ham shanks or hocks**
- **German-style mustard (optional)**

Make-ahead steps: Sort peas and discard any debris; rinse well.

In an 8- to 10-quart pan, combine peas, 3 quarts of the water, onions, carrots, marjoram, and ham. Bring to a boil over medium-high heat; reduce heat, cover, and simmer, stirring occasionally, until peas are soft enough to mash and meat pulls away easily from bone (about 3 hours).

Lift out ham and pull off meat. Discard bone, skin, and fat; tear meat into bite-size chunks. Return to pan. Let cool; cover and refrigerate for up to 5 days. (Or freeze for up to 12 months. Thaw overnight in refrigerator; or defrost in a microwave following manufacturer's directions.)

To serve: Reheat, stirring occasionally, over medium heat until hot (about 20 minutes). Soup will be quite thick; thin with water, if desired. Ladle into bowls and, if desired, offer with mustard. Makes 16 servings (about 4 quarts).

Golden Garden Soup

Initial preparation: About 45 minutes
Storage time: 1 day in refrigerator; 12 months in freezer
Final preparation: Garnish

Per serving: 85 calories, 3 g protein, 9 g carbohydrates, 5 g total fat, 1 mg cholesterol, 413 mg sodium

Rich in taste but not in calories, this velvety buttermilk soup is thickened with puréed vegetables. For a sophisticated lunch, serve it cold, topped with tomato slices and basil.

- 2 **tablespoons salad oil**
- 1 **large onion, chopped**
- 2 **medium-size pear-shaped tomatoes, chopped**
- 1½ **pounds yellow crookneck squash (about 5 medium-size)**
- 3 **cups regular-strength chicken broth**
- 1 **cup buttermilk**
- ¼ **cup loosely packed fresh basil leaves, minced**
- **Basil sprig**
- 1 **or 2 tomato slices (optional)**

Make-ahead steps: Heat oil in a 4- to 5-quart pan over medium heat. When oil is hot, add onion and cook, stirring occasionally, until slightly soft (about 5 minutes). Add chopped tomatoes and continue to cook, stirring often, until tomatoes are soft and fall apart (about 5 more minutes).

Trim and discard ends of squash. Chop squash and add to pan with broth. Bring to a boil over high heat; reduce heat, cover, and simmer until squash is very tender when pierced (about 15 minutes).

In a blender or food processor, combine broth mixture with buttermilk; whirl until puréed.

Stir in minced basil. Cover and refrigerate for up to 1 day. (Or freeze for up to 12 months. Thaw overnight in refrigerator; or defrost in a microwave following manufacturer's directions.)

To serve: Pour into a large tureen. Garnish with basil sprig and if desired, tomato slices. Makes 8 servings.

Dramatic strokes of creamed chile and cilantro lend intriguing flavor and color to Grilled Corn Soup (recipe on facing page). Make the mild corn bisque before your guests arrive for a special evening.

Red Onion Borscht

Initial preparation: About 45 minutes
Storage time: 2 days in refrigerator; 10 months in freezer
Final preparation: About 25 minutes

Per serving: 153 calories, 4 g protein, 18 g carbohydrates, 8 g total fat, 16 mg cholesterol, 829 mg sodium

When fortified with shredded beets, red onions and broth produce a hearty borscht. Slow cooking brings out the onions' natural sweetness.

- ¼ cup butter or margarine
- ½ pound beets, peeled and shredded
- ½ cup red wine vinegar
- 4 large red onions (3 to 3½ lbs. *total*), thinly sliced
- 2½ tablespoons all-purpose flour
- 6 cups regular-strength chicken broth
- ⅓ cup port (optional) Sour cream

Make-ahead steps: In a 5- to 6-quart pan, melt butter over medium heat. Add beets, vinegar, and all but ⅓ cup of the onions (reserve remainder for garnish); cook, stirring often, until onions are very soft (about 20 minutes). Stir in flour and broth. Let cool; cover and refrigerate for up to 2 days. (Or freeze for up to 10 months. Thaw overnight in refrigerator; or defrost in a microwave following manufacturer's directions.)

To serve: Reheat, stirring occasionally, over medium heat just until hot (about 25 minutes); add port, if desired. Garnish individual servings with sour cream and reserved onions. Makes 8 servings.

Pictured on facing page

Grilled Corn Soup

Initial preparation: About 1 hour
Storage time: 1 day in refrigerator; 10 months in freezer
Final preparation: About 20 minutes; or garnish

Per serving: 263 calories, 7 g protein, 30 g carbohydrates, 15 g total fat, 40 mg cholesterol, 809 mg sodium

Bold streaks of color—cilantro green and chile red—decorate and season this simple but dramatic dish.

- Chile Cream (recipe follows)
- Cilantro Cream (recipe follows)
- 4 large ears corn
- 3 cups regular-strength chicken broth
- 1 large carrot, peeled and chopped
- 1 small stalk celery, chopped
- 1 small onion, chopped
- 2 cloves garlic
- 1 fresh jalapeño chile, stemmed, seeded, and chopped
- ½ cup whipping cream

Make-ahead steps: Prepare Chile Cream and Cilantro Cream.

Grill corn in a covered barbecue above a solid bed of medium-hot coals until corn is lightly browned on all sides (about 15 minutes). Remove from grill and let cool. Cut corn kernels from cob; set aside.

Bring broth, carrot, celery, onion, garlic, and chile to a boil over medium-high heat; reduce heat and simmer, uncovered, for 5 minutes. Add corn, cover, and simmer until vegetables are tender (5 to 10 more minutes). In a blender, whirl soup, a portion at a time, until smoothly puréed. Pour through a fine wire strainer set over a bowl.

Stir in cream. Cool; cover and refrigerate for up to 1 day. (Or freeze for up to 10 months. Thaw overnight in refrigerator; or defrost in a microwave following manufacturer's directions.)

To serve: Serve at room temperature or heat, stirring, over low heat until hot (about 20 minutes). Drizzle chile and cilantro creams over each serving. Makes 4 servings.

Chile Cream. Bake 1 **dry ancho or California chile** in a 400° oven until lightly toasted (about 1 minute). Remove and discard seeds. Crumble chile into a bowl; cover with 1 cup **hot water** and soak until soft (about 10 minutes). Drain.

Whirl chile and 2 tablespoons *each* **milk** and **sour cream** in a blender until puréed. If needed, add more milk until mixture reaches consistency of soup. Cover and refrigerate for up to 1 day.

Cilantro Cream. Whirl ½ cup lightly packed **fresh cilantro (coriander) leaves,** 1 teaspoon **milk,** and 1½ tablespoons **sour cream** in a blender until puréed. If needed, add more milk until mixture reaches consistency of soup. Cover and refrigerate for up to 1 day.

Sauces & Salsas

Whether you say it in English or Spanish, the right sauce (or *salsa*) adds excitement to any meal. The sauces below—from the elegant Béarnaise to our easy Red Bell Pepper—can transform a simple dish into something very special.

Béarnaise Sauce

1 tablespoon minced shallots or green onion
1 teaspoon dry tarragon
3 tablespoons white wine vinegar
1 egg or 3 egg yolks
1 teaspoon Dijon mustard
1 tablespoon lemon juice or white wine vinegar
1 cup (½ lb.) hot melted butter or margarine

Make-ahead steps: In a 1-quart or smaller pan, combine shallots, tarragon, and vinegar. Simmer, uncovered, over medium heat until mixture is reduced to 2 tablespoons.

In a blender or food processor, combine egg, mustard, and lemon juice; whirl to blend. Add shallot mixture. With motor running, add butter, pouring in a slow stream at first and then more rapidly as mixture begins to thicken. Pour into a 1-quart container; cover and refrigerate for up to 1 week.

To serve: Bring to room temperature, stirring often until softened. Place container in hot water; stir just until sauce is warm. Makes 1¾ cups.

Per tablespoon: 62 calories, .28 g protein, .20 g carbohydrates, 7 g total fat, 28 mg cholesterol, 75 mg sodium

Garden Marinara Sauce

¼ cup olive oil
3 large onions, chopped
3 or 4 cloves garlic, minced or pressed
6 pounds tomatoes, cored, peeled, and chopped
1 cup lightly packed fresh basil leaves, finely chopped
½ tablespoon sugar
Salt and pepper

Make-ahead steps: Heat oil in a 6- to 8-quart pan over medium heat. When oil is hot, add onions and garlic; cook, stirring often, until onions are golden brown (about 25 minutes). Add tomatoes and basil. Cook, uncovered, stirring occasionally, until sauce is reduced to 8 cups (45 minutes to 1 hour). Add sugar; season to taste with salt and pepper. Cover and refrigerate for up to 1 week. (Or freeze for up to 6 months. Thaw overnight in refrigerator; or defrost in a microwave following manufacturer's directions.)

To serve: Bring to a boil over medium heat. Makes about 2 quarts.

Per ¼ cup: 38 calories, .96 g protein, 5 g carbohydrates, 2 g total fat, 0 mg cholesterol, 7 mg sodium

Red Bell Pepper Sauce

2 tablespoons salad oil
2 medium-size red bell peppers, seeded and chopped
2 medium-size onions, chopped
3 tablespoons shiro (white) miso or 2 tablespoons soy sauce

Make-ahead steps: Heat oil in a 10- to 12-inch frying pan over medium-high heat. When oil is hot, add bell peppers and onions; cook, stirring occasionally, until onions begin to brown (about 15 minutes). In a food processor or blender, combine bell peppers and onions with miso. Whirl until smoothly puréed. Cover and refrigerate for up to 5 days. (Or freeze for up to 2 months. Thaw overnight in refrigerator; or defrost in a microwave following manufacturer's directions.)

To serve: Bring to room temperature. Makes about 1¾ cups.

Per tablespoon: 16 calories, .31 g protein, 1 g carbohydrates, 1 g total fat, 0 mg cholesterol, 67 mg sodium

Spiced Yogurt-Cashew Sauce

⅔ cup roasted salted cashews
2 tablespoons butter or margarine
2 large onions, thinly sliced
1 tablespoon minced fresh ginger
2 cloves garlic, minced or pressed
¼ teaspoon ground turmeric
⅛ to ¼ teaspoon ground red pepper (cayenne)
1 tablespoon all-purpose flour
1⅓ cups regular-strength chicken broth
1 cup plain yogurt
Salt and pepper

Make-ahead steps: In a blender, whirl cashews until finely ground; set aside.

In a 10- to 12-inch frying pan, melt butter over medium heat; add onions and cook, stirring often, until very soft and light gold (about 20 minutes). Add ginger, garlic, turmeric, and ground red pepper; cook, stirring, for 1 minute. Stir in flour. Add broth and bring to a boil, stirring. Add ground nuts and yogurt. Continue to cook, stirring, until sauce is hot. Season to taste with salt and pepper. Let cool; cover and refrigerate for up to 2 days.

To serve: Reheat, stirring, over medium heat until hot. Makes about 3⅓ cups.

Per tablespoon: 20 calories, .61 g protein, 1 g carbohydrates, 1 g total fat, 1 mg cholesterol, 43 mg sodium

Mustard Cream

- 2 egg yolks
- 1 tablespoon sugar
- ¼ cup Dijon mustard
- 2 tablespoons white wine vinegar
- 1 tablespoon water
- 1½ tablespoons prepared horseradish
- 1 tablespoon butter or margarine
- ½ cup whipping cream

Make-ahead steps: In top of a double boiler, beat together egg yolks, sugar, mustard, vinegar, water, horseradish, and butter. Place over simmering water and cook, stirring, until mixture thickens (3 to 5 minutes). Place mixture over cold water and stir until thoroughly cooled.

Beat whipping cream until it holds stiff peaks. Fold mustard mixture into whipped cream until completely blended. Cover and refrigerate for up to 1 week. Makes about 1½ cups.

Per tablespoon: 29 calories, .34 g protein, 1 g carbohydrates, 3 g total fat, 30 mg cholesterol, 83 mg sodium

Mediterranean Olive Salsa

- ¼ cup lime juice
- ¼ cup minced shallots or green onions (including tops)
- 3 tablespoons olive oil or salad oil
- 1 tablespoon minced fresh tarragon or 1½ teaspoons dry tarragon
- ½ teaspoon Dijon mustard
- 8 canned anchovy fillets, drained and minced
- 1 medium-size red, yellow, or green bell pepper, seeded and diced
- 1 can (6 oz.) pitted black ripe olives, drained and coarsely chopped

Make-ahead steps: In a bowl, stir together lime juice, shallots, oil, tarragon, mustard, anchovies, bell pepper, and olives. Cover and refrigerate for up to 2 days. (Or freeze for up to 4 months. Thaw overnight in refrigerator; or defrost in a microwave following manufacturer's directions.)

To serve: Bring to room temperature. Makes 2½ cups.

Per tablespoon: 20 calories, .32 g protein, .51 g carbohydrates, 2 g total fat, .44 mg cholesterol, 64 mg sodium

Chorreada Salsa

- ¼ cup olive oil
- 1 large onion, chopped
- 1 fresh jalapeño or serrano chile, stemmed, seeded, and chopped
- ½ teaspoon *each* ground turmeric and ground cumin
- 2 cups cored, chopped tomatoes
- 2 tablespoons chopped fresh cilantro (coriander)
- ¾ cup whipping cream
- 1 cup (4 oz.) shredded Münster, fontina, or jack cheese
  Salt and pepper

Make-ahead steps: Heat oil in a 3- to 4-quart pan over medium heat. When oil is hot, add onion, chile,

turmeric, and cumin. Cook, stirring, until onion is soft (about 10 minutes). Add tomatoes; reduce heat and simmer, uncovered, stirring occasionally, until liquid has evaporated (15 to 20 minutes).

Reduce heat to low. Stir in cilantro, cream, and cheese. Continue to cook, stirring, until cheese is melted and well blended. Season to taste with salt and pepper. Cover and refrigerate for up to 1 day.

To serve: Reheat, stirring, over low heat just until warm. Makes about 2¼ cups.

Per tablespoon: 43 calories, .96 g protein, .98 g carbohydrates, 4 g total fat, 9 mg cholesterol, 22 mg sodium

Tropical Fruit Salsa

- 1 medium-size firm-ripe mango
- 1 cup *each* diced fresh pineapple and honeydew melon
- ½ cup diced red bell pepper
- ⅓ cup seasoned rice wine vinegar (or ⅓ cup rice wine vinegar and 1 tablespoon sugar)
- 2 tablespoons minced fresh cilantro (coriander) leaves
- ½ teaspoon crushed dried hot red chiles
- 2 large kiwi fruit

Make-ahead steps: Peel mango and cut fruit away from pit; cut into ½-inch cubes. In a bowl, mix mango, pineapple, melon, bell pepper, vinegar, cilantro, and chiles. Cover and refrigerate for up to 2 days. (Or freeze for up to 2 months. Thaw overnight in refrigerator; or defrost in a microwave following manufacturer's directions.)

To serve: Peel kiwi, cut into about ¼-inch cubes, and add to salsa. Makes about 4 cups.

Per tablespoon: 7 calories, .04 g protein, 2 g carbohydrates, .02 g total fat, 0 mg cholesterol, .70 mg sodium

Carrot Yogurt Soup

Initial preparation: *About 30 minutes*
Storage time: *1 day in refrigerator; 4 months in freezer*
Final preparation: *About 20 minutes; or garnish*

Per serving: 250 calories, 9 g protein, 22 g carbohydrates, 16 g total fat, 3 mg cholesterol, 934 mg sodium

Golden puréed carrots blend with yogurt in this refreshingly cool, yet spicy, soup.

> **Carrot Curls (directions follow), optional**
> 2 **tablespoons salad oil**
> 1 **large onion, chopped**
> 1 **clove garlic, minced or pressed**
> 1 **teaspoon** *each* **curry powder and all-purpose flour**
> 3 **cups regular-strength chicken broth**
> 3 **large carrots, peeled and sliced**
> 1 **cup plain yogurt**
> **Salt**
> **Ground red pepper (cayenne)**
> ⅓ **cup chopped salted roasted peanuts**

Make-ahead steps: Prepare Carrot Curls, if desired.

Heat oil in a 3- to 4-quart pan over medium heat. When oil is hot, add onion and garlic; cook, stirring, until onion is soft (about 10 minutes). Add curry powder and flour; continue to cook, stirring, for about 30 seconds. Add broth and carrots. Cover and simmer until carrots are tender when pierced (15 to 20 minutes).

In a blender or food processor, whirl the mixture, about half at a time, with ¾ cup of the yogurt until smoothly puréed. Season to taste with salt and ground red pepper. Let cool; cover and refrigerate for up to 1 day. (Or freeze for up to 4 months.

Thaw overnight in refrigerator; or defrost in a microwave following manufacturer's directions.)

To serve: Serve at room temperature or heat over medium heat until hot (about 20 minutes). Garnish with peanuts, carrot curls, if desired, and remaining yogurt. Makes 4 servings.

Carrot Curls. Peel 1 large **carrot.** Cut lengthwise in thin strips. Loosely curl strips and immerse in ice water until crisp (about 10 minutes). Refrigerate for up to 1 day. Lift out curls and drain.

Hot Ginger Pear Soup

Initial preparation: *About 1 hour*
Storage time: *2 days in refrigerator; 6 months in freezer*
Final preparation: *About 20 minutes; or garnish*

Per serving: 227 calories, 1 g protein, 58 g carbohydrates, 1 g total fat, 0 mg cholesterol, .44 mg sodium

A day or two in advance, prepare the soup using firm-ripe Bartlett pears. Offer hot as a first course or cold as a dessert.

> 3 **pounds firm-ripe Bartlett pears, peeled, halved, and cored**
> 3 **cups water**
> 3 **tablespoons sugar**
> 1 **vanilla bean (6 to 7 inches long) or 1 teaspoon vanilla**
> 1 **cinnamon stick**
> 3 **whole cloves**
> 2 **slices fresh ginger (***each*** about ⅛ inch thick and 1 inch across)**
> **Mint sprigs**

Make-ahead steps: In a 3- to 4-quart pan, combine pears, water, sugar, vanilla bean (split lengthwise), cinnamon stick (2 or 3 inches long), cloves, and ginger. Bring to a boil over high heat; reduce heat, cover, and simmer for 30 minutes. Lift out pears and ginger with a slotted spoon and place in a blender. Whirl until smooth; set aside.

Meanwhile, bring liquid in pan to a boil; cook, uncovered, over high heat until reduced to 2 cups (about 10 minutes). Remove from heat. Remove and discard cinnamon, cloves, and vanilla bean. Stir pear purée into liquid. If

necessary, add water to make 6 cups. Let cool; cover and refrigerate for up to 2 days. (Or freeze for up to 6 months. Thaw overnight in refrigerator; or defrost in a microwave following manufacturer's directions.)

To serve: Reheat, stirring occasionally, over medium heat until hot (about 20 minutes), or serve cold. Garnish with mint sprigs. Makes 4 servings.

A velvety, curry-spiced experience, either hot or cold, Carrot Yogurt Soup (recipe on facing page) is garnished with carrot curls, roasted peanuts, and yogurt.

Main Dishes

Beef ■ Veal ■ Pork ■ Lamb ■ Poultry ■ Seafood ■ Eggs & Cheese

From simple family fare to impressive party showpieces, main dishes are the focus of a menu. This chapter features such hearty entrées as Pot Roast with Onions, elegant Pork Loin Stuffed with Two Cheeses, and rustic Dill Lamb & Carrot Stew. Chicken appears boned and stuffed for Broccoli- & Cheese-stuffed Chicken Breasts, or it's cooked with capers, tomatoes, and rice in Arroz con Pollo. For fish fanciers, main dishes include Creamy Scallop Lasagne and tuna with anchovy dressing in Layered Niçoise Salad. Even eggs and cheese yield marvelous main dishes in Poached Eggs & Prosciutto topped with fresh basil mayonnaise or buttery Chard, Feta & Fila Pie.

Pot Roast with Onions

Initial preparation: About 4 hours, plus at least 4 hours for marinating
Storage time: 1 day in refrigerator; 2 weeks in freezer
Final preparation: About 30 minutes

Per serving: 341 calories, 30 g protein, 7 g carbohydrates, 21 g total fat, 91 mg cholesterol, 249 mg sodium

Our marinated beef braises at a leisurely pace, allowing you time to relax before dinner.

- ⅓ **cup Worcestershire**
- 3 **cloves garlic, minced or pressed**
- ¼ **teaspoon pepper**
  4- to 5-pound beef sirloin tip roast
- 3 **tablespoons salad oil**
- 1 **large can (28 oz.) tomatoes**
- 1 **large green bell pepper, seeded and thinly sliced**
- 2 **large onions, thinly sliced**
- ¼ **teaspoon** *each* **dry thyme and dry oregano leaves**
- 2 **bay leaves**

Make-ahead steps: In a 9- by 13-inch pan, mix Worcestershire, garlic, and pepper. Place beef in pan; turn to coat with marinade. Cover and refrigerate for at least 4 hours or for up to 1 day, turning meat occasionally.

Lift out meat; pat dry. Refrigerate marinade for up to 1 day. Heat oil in a 5- to 6-quart pan over medium heat. When oil is hot, add meat and cook, turning occasionally, until browned (about 10 minutes). Add tomatoes (break up with a spoon) and their liquid, bell pepper, onions, thyme, oregano, and bay leaves.

Bring to a boil. Reduce heat, cover, and simmer, turning meat occasionally, until very tender when pierced (about 3½ hours). Let cool; cover and refrigerate for up to 1 day. (Or freeze for up to 2 weeks. Thaw overnight in refrigerator; or defrost in a microwave following manufacturer's directions.)

To serve: Bring sauce with meat to a boil, covered, over medium heat; reduce heat and simmer until meat is hot (about 20 minutes). Lift out meat; let stand for about 5 minutes. Remove strings; slice meat and place on a rimmed platter. Skim fat from sauce. Add marinade to sauce to taste. Bring to a boil and serve in a separate bowl or pour over meat. Makes 10 to 12 servings.

Oven-braised Brisket

Initial preparation: About 3 ¼ hours
Storage time: 1 day
Final preparation: About 35 minutes

Per serving: 284 calories, 24 g protein, 8 g carbohydrates, 17 g total fat, 79 mg cholesterol, 577 mg sodium

Slow cooking lets flavors mingle in this hearty Russian beef brisket, served over sweet onions and sauerkraut.

- 2 **tablespoons salad oil**
  2¾- to 3-pound center-cut piece beef brisket, fat trimmed
- ¼ **cup butter or margarine**
- 4 **large onions, thinly sliced**
- 1 **can or jar (32 oz.) sauerkraut**
- 1¾ **cups regular-strength beef broth**
  Pepper
  Parsley sprigs

Make-ahead steps: Heat 1 tablespoon of the oil in a 5- to 6-quart ovenproof pan over medium heat. When oil is hot, add beef and cook, turning once, until well browned on both sides (about 10 minutes total). Remove from pan; set aside.

Add 2 tablespoons of the butter; remaining 1 tablespoon oil, and onions to pan; cook, stirring occasionally, until onions are very soft (about 20 minutes). Drain sauerkraut; stir into onions along with broth. Set beef on top.

Cover and bake in a 350° oven until meat is very tender when pierced, turning meat several times (about 2½ hours). Let cool; cover and refrigerate for up to 1 day.

To serve: Bring onion mixture to a boil, covered, over medium heat; reduce heat and simmer until meat is hot (about 20 minutes). Lift out meat and cut across grain ½ inch thick. Season onion mixture to taste with pepper; lift out with a slotted spoon, reserving juices, and arrange in center of a large platter. Overlap meat slices on top.

Carefully drain juices from platter and add to juices in pan; boil over high heat until reduced to ¾ cup (about 5 minutes). Add remaining 2 tablespoons butter, stirring until incorporated. Spoon sauce over meat; garnish with parsley. Makes 8 servings.

Need a meaty solution to the dinner debate? Serve Baked Stuffed Flank Steak
Roll (recipe on facing page). With baked potatoes and Summer Squash
Gratin (recipe on page 70), this savory main dish is sure to be a winner.

Pictured on facing page

Baked Stuffed Flank Steak Roll

Initial preparation: *About 30 minutes, plus at least 1 hour for marinating*
Storage time: *1 day in refrigerator; 1 month in freezer*
Final preparation: *About 3¼ hours*

Per serving: 643 calories, 37 g protein, 62 g carbohydrates, 28 g total fat, 99 mg cholesterol, 1,172 mg sodium

Here, we wrap flank steak around a savory filling of sautéed mushrooms to create an attractive meat roll. You can gain an extra head start by marinating the steak for a day before stuffing and baking it.

- ¼ **cup** *each* **lemon juice, soy sauce, and honey**
- 1 **teaspoon dry mustard**
- ½ **teaspoon pepper**
  2-pound flank steak
  Mushroom Stuffing (recipe follows)
- 6 **medium-size russet potatoes (about 3 lbs.** *total***), scrubbed and pierced with a fork**
- 2 **cups regular-strength beef broth**
- 2 **tablespoons cornstarch**
  Parsley sprigs

Make-ahead steps: In a 9- by 13-inch baking pan, mix lemon juice, soy sauce, honey, dry mustard, and pepper. Place flank steak in pan; turn to coat with marinade. Cover and refrigerate for at least 1 hour or until next day, turning meat occasionally. Meanwhile, prepare Mushroom Stuffing.

Lift steak from marinade, brushing excess sauce into pan. Spread stuffing over meat to within 1 inch of edges. Fold ends over stuffing; then roll lengthwise. With cotton string, tie rolled meat in center and at each end. Place steak, seam side down, in pan with marinade; cover tightly with foil. Refrigerate for up to 1 day. (Or freeze for up to 1 month. Thaw overnight in refrigerator; or defrost in a microwave following manufacturer's directions.)

To serve: Bake in center of a 350° oven until very tender when pierced (about 3 hours). About 1 hour before steak is done, place potatoes on rack above meat; bake until tender when pierced.

Using 2 spoons, carefully lift rolled steak and place, seam side down, on a platter; remove string. Drape meat with foil and keep warm.

Carefully skim and discard fat from pan drippings. Stir broth and cornstarch into pan. Bring mixture to a boil, stirring, over high heat.

Cut steak crosswise into 6 equal pieces. Arrange meat and potatoes on 6 dinner plates, garnish with parsley, and serve with sauce. Makes 6 servings.

Mushroom Stuffing. Slice 1 pound **mushrooms.** Chop 1 medium-size **onion.** In a 10- to 12-inch frying pan, melt ¼ cup **butter** or margarine over medium-high heat. Add vegetables and cook, stirring occasionally, until golden brown (about 15 minutes). Stir in ½ cup chopped **parsley.**

Let cool; cover and refrigerate for up to 1 day.

Pictured on page 63

Picnic Caper Loaf

Initial preparation: *About 1¼ hours*
Storage time: *2 days in refrigerator; 1 month in freezer*
Final preparation: *None*

Per serving: 264 calories, 22 g protein, 6 g carbohydrates, 17 g total fat, 100 mg cholesterol, 394 mg sodium

Cold meat loaf becomes a gourmet item when it goes on a picnic. Cut thick slices to make generous sandwiches.

- 2 **pounds lean ground beef**
- ½ **cup dry white wine or regular-strength chicken broth**
- ⅓ **cup** *each* **capers, drained, and quick-cooking rolled oats**
- 1 **clove garlic, minced or pressed**
- 2 **teaspoons green peppercorns, drained and chopped, or ½ teaspoon pepper**
- 4 **teaspoons Dijon mustard**
- ⅓ **cup catsup**
- 1 **large egg**

Make-ahead steps: In a large bowl, mix beef, wine, capers, oats, garlic, peppercorns, mustard, catsup, and egg. Pack mixture into a 4- by 8-inch loaf pan or deep 1½-quart pan. Bake in a 350° oven until meat is no longer pink in center when cut (about 1 hour). Let cool; cover and refrigerate for up to 2 days. (Or freeze for up to 1 month. Thaw overnight in refrigerator; or defrost in a microwave following manufacturer's directions.)

To serve: Discard any solid fat and serve cold. Makes 6 to 8 servings.

Santa Fe Chili with Meat

Initial preparation: About 7 hours
Storage time: 2 days in refrigerator; 2 weeks in freezer
Final preparation: About 1 hour

Per serving: 410 calories, 31 g protein, 17 g carbohydrates, 25 g total fat, 93 mg cholesterol, 525 mg sodium

Slow cooking blends the exuberant seasonings as it also renders the beef meltingly tender in this New Mexican favorite.

Red Chile Sauce (directions follow)
½ cup salad oil or olive oil
2 large onions, chopped
3 cloves garlic, minced or pressed
5 pounds boneless beef steak, cut into 1½-inch cubes
½ cup all-purpose flour
1 tablespoon minced fresh cilantro (coriander) leaves
2 teaspoons *each* ground cumin, ground cloves, and dry oregano leaves
1½ teaspoons *each* dry rosemary and dry tarragon
2 large cans (28 oz. *each*) tomatoes
1 can (14½ oz.) regular-strength beef broth

Make-ahead steps: Prepare Red Chile Sauce; set aside.

Heat oil in a 6- to 8-quart pan over medium heat. When oil is hot, add onions and garlic and cook, stirring often, until onions are soft (about 10 minutes). In a large bowl, sprinkle meat with flour and mix.

Add meat and chile sauce to pan. Cook, stirring, for about 5 minutes. Add cilantro, cumin, cloves, oregano, rosemary, tarragon, tomatoes (break up with a spoon) and their liquid, and broth. Simmer, stirring occasionally, until meat is very tender when pierced (about 6 hours). Cover and refrigerate for up to 2 days. (Or freeze for up to 2 weeks. Thaw overnight in refrigerator; or defrost in a microwave following manufacturer's directions.)

To serve: Reheat, stirring occasionally, over medium heat until hot (about 1 hour). Makes 12 servings.

Red Chile Sauce. Wash 4 ounces (about 15) **dried New Mexico or pasilla chiles.** Remove seeds. In a 2½- to 3-quart pan, combine chiles and 3 cups **water.** Bring to a boil over medium-high heat; reduce heat, cover, and simmer until chiles are very soft (about 30 minutes). Lift out chiles, reserving cooking liquid.

In a blender, whirl chiles (add cooking liquid as needed) until puréed. Rub through a fine wire strainer; discard residue.

Return purée to pan. Boil over high heat, uncovered, stirring often, until reduced to 1 cup.

Shredded Beef Enchiladas

Initial preparation: About 3¼ hours
Storage time: 1 day
Final preparation: About 30 minutes

Per serving: 883 calories, 44 g protein, 37 g carbohydrates, 63 g total fat, 158 mg cholesterol, 1,176 mg sodium

In Mexico, this richly flavored beef is a classic filling for enchiladas with green chiles, sour cream, and jack cheese.

Shredded Beef (recipe follows)
Salad oil
1 small onion, chopped
2 large cans (7 oz. *each*) diced green chiles
½ teaspoon ground cumin
1 tablespoon all-purpose flour
2 cups sour cream
3 cups (¾ lb.) shredded jack cheese
Salt
12 corn tortillas (6- to 7-inch diameter)

Make-ahead steps: Prepare Shredded Beef; set aside.

Heat 2 tablespoons oil in an 8- to 10-inch frying pan over medium heat. When oil is hot, add onion, chiles, and cumin. Cook, stirring occasionally, until onion is soft (about 10 minutes).

Mix in flour; then blend in 1 cup of the sour cream and continue to cook, stirring, until mixture is barely simmering. Remove from heat and blend in 1 cup of the cheese; season to taste with salt. Set aside.

Pour oil to a depth of ½ inch into a 7- to 8-inch frying pan over medium-high heat. When oil is hot, cook tortillas, 1 at a time, until surface bubbles and tortillas are

Continued on next page

still soft (about 5 seconds on each side). Drain on paper towels.

Spoon about ⅓ cup of the chile mixture and ¼ cup of the shredded beef mixture down center of each tortilla; roll to enclose. Set, seam side down, in a shallow 12- by 15-inch baking pan. Cover and refrigerate for up to 1 day.

To serve: Bake, uncovered, in a 375° oven until hot in center (about 25 minutes). Sprinkle remaining 2 cups cheese evenly

on top. Continue baking until cheese is melted (about 5 more minutes). Offer remaining 1 cup sour cream to spoon on individual servings. Makes 6 servings.

Shredded Beef. Trim and discard fat from a 2-pound **boneless beef chuck.** In a 5- to 6-quart pan, combine beef with ¼ cup **water;** cook, covered, over medium heat for 30 minutes. Uncover and continue to cook, turning as needed, until liquid has boiled away and meat is well browned (about 15 minutes).

Lift out meat. To pan, add 3 tablespoons **red wine vinegar;** scrape to loosen browned bits. Stir in 1½ cups **regular-strength beef broth,** 2 tablespoons **chili powder,** and 1 teaspoon **ground cumin.**

Return meat to pan and bring to a boil over medium-high heat; reduce heat, cover, and simmer until meat is very tender and pulls apart easily (about 2 hours). Let cool; then tear into shreds and mix with pan juices.

Pictured on page 7

Brazilian Feijoada with Farofa

Initial preparation: About 4 hours
Storage time: 2 days
Final preparation: About 1 hour

Per serving: 1,119 calories, 61 g protein, 102 g carbohydrates, 53 g total fat, 164 mg cholesterol, 1,414 mg sodium

---

Savory smoked meats and black beans go into this popular party stew, which can be made up to 2 days in advance.

  2½-pound smoked or corned beef tongue
  ½-pound Brazilian carne seca (dried beef) or beef jerky
1½ pounds (3½ cups) dried black beans
  5 pounds lean beef short ribs, trimmed of fat, sawed into 2-inch lengths
  Farofa (recipe follows)
  ½ pound *each* beef link sausage, Polish sausage (kielbasa), and linguisa (Portuguese-style sausage)
  ⅛ pound Canadian bacon, cut into ¼-inch cubes
  2 tablespoons salad oil
  8 cloves garlic, minced or pressed
  2 bay leaves
  2 large onions, chopped
  ⅓ cup minced parsley
  Fresh Salsa (recipe follows)
  Brown Rice (recipe follows)
  Wilted Kale (recipe follows)
  5 oranges, peeled and sliced crosswise

Make-ahead steps: In a 10- to 12-quart pan, cover tongue and carne seca with cold water. Bring to a boil over high heat and drain; repeat.

Sort beans and discard any debris; rinse well. Add to pan with 4½ quarts water and ribs; bring to a boil over high heat. Reduce heat, cover, and simmer until tongue is very tender when pierced (about 2¾ hours). Meanwhile, prepare Farofa.

Add beef, Polish, and linguisa sausages and bacon to pan; simmer until sausages are hot when cut (about 10 more minutes). Skim and discard fat from liquid.

Lift out sausages and cut into 1-inch chunks; arrange on a large ovenproof platter. Lift out tongue. Cut off and discard skin; cut meat into 1-inch chunks and place next to sausages. Lift out ribs and arrange next to tongue. Lift out carne seca; cut into 1- to 2-inch pieces and place on platter with other meats. Let cool.

Ladle 2 quarts of the broth from pan (there will still be broth

on beans); reserve ½ cup for salsa. Save balance for other uses. With a slotted spoon, remove 1½ cups of the beans from pan; set aside.

Heat oil in a 10- to 12-inch frying pan over medium-high heat. When oil is hot, add garlic, bay leaves, and onions. Cook, stirring occasionally, until onions are soft (about 10 minutes).

Add parsley and reserved beans; mash beans with back of a spoon. Continue to cook, stirring, until mixture bubbles. Return bean mixture to large pan. Let cool. Cover and refrigerate meats and bean mixture separately for up to 2 days.

To serve: Prepare Fresh Salsa, Brown Rice, and Wilted Kale; set aside. Bake meat and farofa, covered, in a 350° oven until hot (about 30 minutes). Bring bean mixture to a boil, stirring, over medium-high heat. Pour into a bowl.

Continued on next page

Arrange farofa, salsa, rice, kale, and oranges in separate dishes and offer to spoon over individual servings. Ladle bean mixture over meat. Makes 12 to 14 servings.

Farofa. In a 12- to 14-inch frying pan, melt 3 tablespoons **butter** or margarine over medium-high heat. Add 1 large **onion,** chopped, and cook until soft (about 10 minutes). Add 2½ cups (1 lb.) **manioc flour** or farina. Cook, stirring often, until manioc is golden (about 20 minutes).

In a bowl, mash 2 medium-size **bananas** until fairly smooth.

Add 1 large **egg;** mix until blended. Add to manioc mixture and stir to coat. Let cool. Place in a shallow 2½-quart baking pan; cover and refrigerate for up to 2 days.

Fresh Salsa. Dice 1 pound **tomatoes.** Combine in a bowl with ½ cup reserved **bean broth;** 1 large **onion,** minced; 1 large can (7 oz.) **diced green chiles;** ¼ cup minced **parsley;** 2 tablespoons *each* **lemon juice** and **white wine vinegar;** and ½ teaspoon **pepper.**

Brown Rice. In a 3- to 4-quart pan, bring 4½ cups **water** and, if desired, 1 teaspoon **salt** to a boil

over high heat. Add 2 cups **long-grain brown rice.** Reduce heat, cover, and simmer until rice is tender to bite (about 40 minutes).

Wilted Kale. Cut off and discard stems from 2½ pounds **kale.** Wash leaves and chop. In a 5- to 6-quart pan, bring 2 cups **water** to a boil over high heat; add kale and cook, stirring, until leaves are wilted (about 3 minutes).

Pictured on facing page

Mustard-glazed Veal Strips

Initial preparation: *About 1½ hours*
Storage time: *1 day*
Final preparation: *About 45 minutes and/or garnish*

Per serving: 617 calories, 38 g protein, 29 g carbohydrates, 40 g total fat, 129 mg cholesterol, 1,033 mg sodium

---

Impress your guests with this succulent oven-braised veal, glazed with a honey and mustard sauce. It's easy when you get a head start.

> **Mustard Sauce (recipe follows)**
> **2 pounds boneless veal stew meat**
> **About 3 tablespoons salad oil**
> **2 medium-size avocados**
> **1 large papaya**
> **2 tablespoons lime or lemon juice**
> **1 quart watercress sprigs, washed and crisped**
> **Lime or lemon wedges**

Make-ahead steps: Prepare Mustard Sauce; set aside.

Slice veal across grain into ¼-inch strips. Heat 1 tablespoon of the oil in a 10- to 12-inch frying pan over high heat. When oil is

hot, add about a third of the veal strips. Cook, stirring, until lightly browned, (3 to 4 minutes). With a slotted spoon, remove cooked veal from pan. Repeat two more times, adding more oil as needed.

In a shallow 2- to 2½-quart pan or casserole, mix meat with sauce. Cover and bake in a 325° oven for 1 hour.

Uncover and continue baking, stirring occasionally, until meat is tender when pierced and sauce clings to meat (about 15 more minutes; coating on meat should be moist, with little liquid left in pan). Let cool; cover and refrigerate for up to 1 day.

To serve: To serve at room temperature, remove meat from refrigerator about 1 hour before serving. To serve hot, cover and bake in a 325° oven until hot (about 40 minutes), stirring in several tablespoons water to keep coating moist, if necessary.

Pit and peel avocados and papaya and slice lengthwise into ¼-inch wedges. Coat avocados with lime juice to preserve color.

Place fans of alternating avocado and papaya wedges on 4 or 5 dinner plates; then add a bed of watercress at base of each fan. Spoon meat onto watercress and serve with lime wedges. Makes 4 or 5 servings.

Mustard Sauce. Combine 1 small **onion,** chopped; ⅓ cup **Dijon mustard;** 3 tablespoons **honey;** 2 tablespoons **soy sauce;** 1 tablespoon **raspberry vinegar** or red wine vinegar; 1 tablespoon chopped **fresh rosemary** or 2 teaspoons dry rosemary; 1 tablespoon finely chopped **fresh ginger;** and ¼ teaspoon **coarsely ground black pepper.** Mix until blended.

A feast for eyes and palate, tender Mustard-glazed Veal Strips (recipe on
facing page) is accented by fresh rosemary. Watercress, papaya, and avocado
add extra color and flavor.

Poached Veal with Tuna Sauce

Initial preparation: About 2 hours
Storage time: Poached veal: 1 day; sauce: 1 week
Final preparation: Garnish

Per serving: 402 calories, 31 g protein, .63 g carbohydrates, 30 g total fat, 147 mg cholesterol, 207 mg sodium

In this Italian classic, a rich tuna sauce enhances tender boneless veal. Perfect for a summer party, the meat is poached in advance in white wine. When ready, simply garnish and serve.

Tuna Sauce (recipe follows)
4- to 5-pound veal leg or shoulder, boned, rolled, and tied
1½ cups dry white wine
1 large carrot, sliced
1 large stalk celery, sliced
1 small onion, chopped
1 bay leaf
Parsley sprigs
1 clove garlic, minced or pressed
Lemon slices, anchovy fillets, ripe olives, and capers

Make-ahead steps: Prepare Tuna Sauce.

In a 5- to 6-quart pan, combine veal, wine, carrot, celery, onion, bay leaf, 6 sprigs of the parsley, and garlic. Add just enough water to barely cover meat. If desired, insert a meat thermometer into thickest part of meat. Bring to a boil over medium-high heat; reduce heat, cover, and simmer until meat is easily pierced with a fork or meat thermometer registers 170°F (1½ to 2 hours). Let meat cool in cooking liquid.

Remove meat from liquid; slice thinly. Pour a third of the sauce into a large shallow serving dish. Arrange meat slices on top and spoon over remaining sauce. Cover and refrigerate for at least 2 hours or for up to 1 day.

To serve: Garnish with lemon slices, anchovies, olives, capers, and remaining parsley sprigs. Makes about 12 servings.

Tuna Sauce. Drain oil from 1 small can (about 3 oz.) **tuna** into a measuring cup. Add enough **olive oil** or salad oil to make 1 cup.

In a blender or food processor, combine tuna, 5 **anchovy fillets**, 3 tablespoons **lemon juice**, 2 **eggs**, and 1½ tablespoons drained **capers;** whirl until smooth. Gradually add oil in a thin, steady stream until mixture is thick and well blended. Cover and refrigerate for up to 1 week.

Hearty Lasagne Bolognese

Initial preparation: About 1½ hours
Storage time: Sauces: 2 days; lasagne: 1 day
Final preparation: About 1½ hours

Per serving: 645 calories, 28 g protein, 47 g carbohydrates, 38 g total fat, 123 mg cholesterol, 826 mg sodium

This subtle Northern Italian lasagne blends pasta with an eloquent veal sauce, a rich cream sauce, and two kinds of cheese. If you wish, prepare both sauces well ahead of assembling the lasagne.

Veal Sauce (recipe follows)
Cream Sauce (recipe follows)
1 package (1 lb.) lasagne noodles
1 cup (about 5 oz.) grated Parmesan cheese
½ pound thinly sliced mozzarella cheese

Make-ahead steps: Prepare Veal Sauce and Cream Sauce.

In a 6- to 8-quart pan, cook noodles in boiling salted water, following package directions, until barely tender to bite; drain. Overlapping strips slightly, arrange in a single layer over bottom and about 1 inch up sides of a buttered 9- by 13-inch baking pan or shallow 3-quart casserole.

Spread with 1 cup each of the veal and cream sauces. Sprinkle with a third of the Parmesan cheese. Top with a layer of pasta, 1 more cup each of the veal and cream sauces, and half the mozzarella. Repeat entire process; sprinkle with remaining Parmesan cheese. Cover and refrigerate for up to 1 day.

To serve: Bake, uncovered, in a 400° oven until lightly browned and hot in center (about 1 hour). Let stand for about 30 minutes before cutting; lift out portions with a wide spatula. Makes 10 servings.

Continued on next page

Veal Sauce. In a 10- to 12-inch frying pan, heat 2 tablespoons **butter** or margarine and 2 tablespoons **olive oil** or salad oil over medium heat until melted. Add ½ cup *each* finely chopped **onion, celery,** and **carrot.** Cook, stirring, until onion is soft (about 10 minutes). Crumble in 1 pound **ground veal** and cook, stirring, until meat is no longer pink (about 5 minutes). Increase heat to medium-high and add 1 cup **dry white wine;** bring to a boil, stirring, and cook until wine has evaporated.

Reduce heat and add 1 can (15 oz.) **pear-shaped tomatoes** (break up with a spoon) and their liquid, 2 tablespoons **tomato paste,** and ½ cup **whipping cream.** Simmer, uncovered, stirring often, until sauce is reduced to 4 cups (about 15 minutes). Let cool; if made ahead, cover and refrigerate for up to 2 days.

Cream Sauce. In a 2- to 2½-quart pan, melt ½ cup (¼ lb.) **butter** or margarine over medium heat. Add ½ cup **all-purpose flour** and cook, stirring, until mixture turns light golden. Remove from heat and mix in 2 cups *each* **regular-strength chicken broth** and **half-and-half.** Increase heat to high and bring to a boil, stirring. Season to taste with **ground nutmeg.** Let cool; if made ahead, cover and refrigerate for up to 2 days.

Black Bean Cassoulet

Initial preparation: *About 3 hours*
Storage time: *3 days in refrigerator; 1 month in freezer*
Final preparation: *About 1 hour*

Per serving: 703 calories, 53 g protein, 43 g carbohydrates, 35 g total fat, 153 mg cholesterol, 1,079 mg sodium

Traditional French cassoulet dishes up the unexpected when black beans are substituted for white. For your convenience, most of the preparation can be done up to 3 days in advance.

- **3 large onions, unpeeled**
- **¼ pound bacon, chopped**
- **2 tablespoons coarsely chopped fresh ginger**
- **1 fresh jalapeño chile, stemmed, seeded, and chopped**
- **1½ tablespoons dry oregano leaves**
- **1 tablespoon *each* dry thyme leaves and cumin seeds**
- **4 cloves garlic, minced or pressed**
- **1½ pounds dried black beans**
- **2 pounds boneless lean pork (such as pork shoulder or butt), cut into 3-inch cubes**
  About 1¾ quarts regular-strength chicken broth
- **10 chicken thighs (about 3½ lbs. *total*)**
- **1 pound mild Italian sausages**
- **¼ cup butter or margarine**
- **¾ cup coarse soft bread crumbs**
- **¼ cup finely chopped fresh cilantro (coriander) leaves**

Make-ahead steps: Peel and coarsely chop 1 of the onions. In a 6- to 8-quart pan, combine chopped onion and bacon over medium heat. Cook, stirring occasionally, until onion is golden (about 15 minutes). Add ginger, chile, oregano, thyme, cumin seeds, and half the garlic. Continue to cook, stirring, until garlic is soft (about 2 more minutes).

Sort beans and discard any debris; rinse well. Add to pan with pork and enough of the broth to cover meat and beans (about 1½ quarts). Bring to a boil; reduce heat, cover, and simmer, stirring occasionally, until pork is very tender when pierced and beans mash easily (about 2½ hours). With 2 forks, shred pork in pan.

Meanwhile, place remaining 2 onions in a 9-inch square baking pan. Bake in a 350° oven until soft when pressed (about 1 hour). Let cool; peel and quarter.

At same time, arrange chicken, skin sides up, and sausages in a single layer in a 10- by 15-inch pan. Bake in a 350° oven until meat near thighbone is no longer pink when slashed (about 40 minutes). Cut sausages diagonally into ⅜-inch slices.

In a 10- to 12-inch frying pan, melt butter over medium-high heat. Add bread crumbs and remaining garlic. Cook, stirring, until crumbs are lightly browned (about 3 minutes). Set aside.

Place bean mixture in a shallow 6- to 7-quart baking pan and top with onions, chicken, and sausages. Let cool; cover and refrigerate cassoulet, crumbs, and remaining broth separately for up to 3 days. (Or freeze for up to 1 month. Thaw overnight in refrigerator; or defrost in a microwave following manufacturer's directions.)

To serve: Add 1 cup of the remaining broth to cassoulet. Sprinkle with crumbs. Bake, uncovered, in a 350° oven until hot in center (about 1 hour). Sprinkle with cilantro. Makes 10 to 12 servings.

Main Dishes/Pork **33**

Fit for a king, Sausage & Cheese Bells (recipe on facing page) are crowned
by their own stem caps. Italian Garden Salad (recipe on page 61) is
an appetizing accompaniment to the hearty stuffed peppers.

Pork Loin Stuffed with Two Cheeses

Initial preparation: *About 1¾ hours*
Storage time: *1 day*
Final preparation: *None*

Per serving: 617 calories, 33 g protein, 2 g carbohydrates, 52 g total fat, 156 mg cholesterol, 240 mg sodium

Slices of this handsome stuffed roast make a tempting center-piece at a springtime feast. Grape leaves encase the creamy cheese mixture that enriches the roast's center. Serve the meat at room temperature to assure that the fill-ing will stay firm when the roast is cut.

¼ pound (½ cup) *each* **cream cheese and ripened or unripened goat cheese (such as Montrachet or Bûcheron)**
1 teaspoon ground sage
½ teaspoon dry thyme leaves
1 boned pork loin end roast (about 3 lbs.)
12 to 15 large canned grape leaves, drained
Fresh thyme sprigs (optional)

Make-ahead steps: In a bowl, thoroughly blend cream cheese, goat cheese, ½ teaspoon of the sage, and ¼ teaspoon of the dry thyme; set aside.

Open roast and lay flat, fat side down. Cover with plastic wrap and pound with a flat mallet until roast measures 9 by 11 inches. Lay a double layer of grape leaves down center; extend leaves 3 to 4 inches beyond roast at each end.

Spoon cheese mixture down center of leaves; fold ends and sides over filling. Roll meat around filling to enclose firmly but not tightly; tie.

Place roast, fat side up, in a 9- by 13-inch pan. Rub remaining ½ teaspoon sage and ¼ teaspoon

dry thyme on roast. If desired, rub also with fresh thyme. Insert a meat thermometer into thickest part of meat (not filling). Roast, uncovered, in a 375° oven until thermometer registers 170°F (about 1¼ hours). Let cool; cover and refrigerate for up to 1 day.

To serve: About 1 hour before serv-ing, remove meat from refrig-erator; serve at room temperature. Makes 8 servings.

Sausage & Cheese Bells

Initial preparation: *About 30 minutes*
Storage time: *1 day*
Final preparation: *About 40 minutes*

Per serving: 500 calories, 27 g protein, 13 g carbohydrates, 38 g total fat, 105 mg cholesterol, 1,010 mg sodium

Vivid yellow bell peppers make crisp and colorful containers for our filling of mild Italian sausages and Münster cheese.

6 medium-size yellow bell peppers (about 2 lbs. *total***)**
1½ pounds mild Italian sausages, casings removed
2 large onions, sliced
3 cloves garlic, minced or pressed
¼ teaspoon crushed dried hot red chiles
¾ cup chopped parsley
½ pound Münster cheese, cut into ½- inch cubes

Make-ahead steps: Cut off stem ends of peppers and reserve caps; remove seeds. In a 6- to 8-quart pan, bring 3 to 4 quarts water to a boil over high heat. Add peppers and cook for 2 minutes. Lift out and plunge into cold water to cool; drain and set aside.

Break sausages into chunks and place in a 10- to 12-inch frying pan. Cook, stirring, over medium heat until lightly browned (about 10 minutes); lift out. Discard all but 2 tablespoons of the fat.

Add onions and garlic to pan; cook, stirring, over medium heat until onions are soft (about 10

minutes). Stir in chiles, parsley, and sausages; let cool. Lightly mix in cheese.

Fill peppers equally with sau-sage mixture; place in a shallow 1½-quart baking pan. Cover and refrigerate for up to 1 day.

To serve: Bake, uncovered, in a 350° oven for 25 minutes. Top with stem caps and continue baking until hot (15 more minutes). Makes 6 servings.

Dill Lamb & Carrot Stew

Initial preparation: About 2½ hours
Storage time: 2 days
Final preparation: About 25 minutes

Per serving: 441 calories, 44 g protein, 11 g carbohydrates, 24 g total fat, 181 mg cholesterol, 184 mg sodium

Braised to succulence in red wine with carrots and onions, dill-seasoned lamb makes an extraordinary springtime stew. Cream adds a rich finish to this aromatic make-ahead entrée.

> **3** pounds boneless lean lamb stew meat, cut into 1½- to 2-inch cubes
> About **2** cups dry red wine
> **½** cup chopped fresh dill or **1** teaspoon dill weed
> **4** small onions, peeled and cut into quarters
> **6** medium-size carrots, cut into 2-inch lengths
> **½** cup whipping cream
> Salt and pepper

Make-ahead steps: In a 5- to 6-quart pan, combine lamb and ½ cup of the wine. Bring to a boil over medium-high heat; reduce heat, cover, and simmer for 30 minutes. Uncover and cook until liquid boils away; continue to cook meat in its own drippings, turning pieces to brown evenly, for about 30 more minutes. Lift out meat and set aside. Skim off fat.

Add dill and 1½ more cups wine to pan; scrape pan to loosen browned bits. Return meat to pan; add onions and carrots. Reduce heat, cover, and simmer, stirring occasionally, until meat is very tender when pierced (about 1 hour); if needed, add more wine to keep liquid ¼ to ½ inch deep.

Add cream and continue to cook, stirring, just until sauce boils. Season to taste with salt and pepper. Let cool; cover and refrigerate for up to 2 days.

To serve: Reheat, stirring occasionally, over low heat until hot (about 25 minutes). Makes 4 to 6 servings.

Lamb & Bean Curry

Initial preparation: About 3½ hours
Storage time: 2 days in refrigerator; 1 month in freezer
Final preparation: About 25 minutes

Per serving: 571 calories, 45 g protein, 45 g carbohydrates, 24 g total fat, 106 mg cholesterol, 1,074 mg sodium

Intriguing seasonings flavor this hearty white bean stew, made with lamb chunks for substance.

> **2** cups (¾ lb.) dried Great Northern beans
> **4** tablespoons salad oil
> **2** pounds boneless lean lamb stew meat, cut into 1½-inch cubes
> **2** large onions, sliced
> **3** cloves garlic, minced or pressed
> **1** tablespoon minced fresh ginger
> **1** tablespoon *each* cumin seeds and mustard seeds
> **2** cinnamon sticks (*each* 3 inches long)
> **3** bay leaves
> **10** small dried hot red chiles
> **½** teaspoon ground cloves
> **1** teaspoon ground cardamom
> **1** tablespoon ground coriander
> **7** cups regular-strength beef broth

Make-ahead steps: Sort beans and discard any debris; rinse well and set aside.

Heat 1 tablespoon of the oil in a 5- to 6-quart pan over high heat. When oil is hot, add half the lamb and cook, stirring, until browned (about 5 minutes). As lamb is cooked, lift out and set aside. Repeat.

Reduce heat to medium; add onions, garlic, ginger, and remaining 3 tablespoons oil. Cook, stirring occasionally, until onions are very soft (about 15 minutes).

Add cumin seeds, mustard seeds, cinnamon, bay leaves, and 4 of the chiles; cook, stirring, for 3 minutes. Add cloves, cardamom, and coriander; continue to cook, stirring, for 1 more minute. Stir in broth, beans, and lamb and any juices.

Bring to a boil over high heat. Reduce heat, cover, and simmer, stirring often, until beans are very tender to bite (about 3 hours). Let cool; cover and refrigerate for up to 2 days. (Or freeze for up to 1 month. Thaw overnight in refrigerator; or defrost in a microwave following manufacturer's directions.)

To serve: Reheat, stirring occasionally, over medium heat until hot (about 25 minutes). Garnish with remaining chiles. Makes 5 or 6 servings.

Simple Stovetop Moussaka

Initial preparation: About 1½ hours
Storage time: 2 days in refrigerator; 2 weeks in freezer
Final preparation: About 25 minutes

Per serving: 340 calories, 15 g protein, 20 g carbohydrates, 23 g total fat, 54 mg cholesterol, 835 mg sodium

Traditionally baked, Middle Eastern moussaka features succulent layers of ground lamb and eggplant. In this streamlined version, the eggplant is browned over direct heat and then simmered in a savory tomato-lamb sauce.

  1 large eggplant (about 2 lbs.)
1½ teaspoons salt
  2 tablespoons olive oil or salad oil
  1 pound lean ground lamb
  1 medium-size onion, chopped
  2 cloves garlic, minced or pressed
  4 medium-size pear-shaped tomatoes (about ¾ lb. *total*), seeded
  1 can (8 oz.) tomato sauce
  3 tablespoons minced parsley
1½ teaspoons cumin seeds
  1 teaspoon crushed dried hot red chiles
  1 package (10 oz.) frozen pearl onions, thawed
    Plain yogurt or sour cream (optional)

Make-ahead steps: Trim off and discard eggplant stem. Cut eggplant into 1-inch cubes and mix with salt; drain in a strainer for 30 minutes to 1 hour. Rinse well under cool running water; drain and pat dry.

Heat oil in a 10- to 12-inch frying pan over medium-high heat. When oil is hot, add eggplant; cook, stirring often, until cubes are lightly browned (6 to 8 minutes).

Add 2 tablespoons water; stir eggplant, quickly cover pan, and continue to cook. About every minute, add another 2 tablespoons water, stirring eggplant and quickly covering pan, until eggplant is very soft when pressed (about 6 more minutes). Transfer to a bowl and set aside.

Add lamb, onion, and garlic to pan; increase heat to high. Cook, stirring, until meat is very well browned (about 8 minutes). Stir in eggplant and any juices, tomatoes, tomato sauce, parsley, cumin seeds, and chiles. Reduce heat, cover, and simmer until flavors are well blended and tomatoes are soft (about 20 minutes).

Gently stir in pearl onions and cook for 1 to 2 more minutes. Let cool; cover and refrigerate for up to 2 days. (Or freeze for up to 2 weeks. Thaw overnight in refrigerator; or defrost in a microwave following manufacturer's directions.)

To serve: Reheat, stirring occasionally, over medium heat until hot (about 25 minutes). Serve with yogurt, if desired. Makes 6 servings.

Pictured on page 95

Armenian Baked Lahmejun

Initial preparation: About 1 hour
Storage time: 1 day
Final preparation: About 15 minutes

Per serving: 511 calories, 37 g protein, 61 g carbohydrates, 13 g total fat, 106 mg cholesterol, 757 mg sodium

This open-faced lamb sandwich is an Armenian answer to the pizza or taco. In our version, the spicy ground lamb is spread on flour tortillas instead of traditional rounds of yeast dough.

  2 medium-size green bell peppers, finely chopped
  1 pound pear-shaped tomatoes, finely chopped
  2 pounds lean ground lamb
  2 cups lightly packed minced parsley
  2 cloves garlic, minced or pressed
  1 can (6 oz.) tomato paste
  2 teaspoons *each* ground allspice, pepper, and paprika
    Salt
 12 flour tortillas (8-inch diameter)
    Condiments (suggestions follow)
    Mint leaves

Make-ahead steps: In a 5- to 6-quart pan, combine bell peppers and tomatoes. Cook, stirring often, over medium heat until vegetables are soft (about 15 minutes). Increase heat to high and continue to cook, stirring often, until most of the liquid has cooked away; take care not to scorch. Let cool.

Continued on next page

In a large bowl, mix vegetable mixture with lamb, parsley, garlic, tomato paste, allspice, pepper, and paprika. Season to taste with salt.

Fill 1 or 2 lightly greased 12- by 15-inch baking sheets with a single layer of tortillas; do not overlap. Spoon about ½ cup of the meat mixture onto each tortilla and spread evenly in a thin layer to within ½ inch of edges.

Bake in a 500° oven until tortilla edges are well browned and meat looks dry (about 8 minutes),

alternating pan positions halfway through baking if using 2 pans. Slide a spatula under hot lahmejun to loosen; let cool in pan for several minutes. Transfer to a flat surface. Repeat until all lahmejun are cooked. With filled sides facing, stack lahmejun in pairs. Wrap airtight and refrigerate for up to 1 day.

To serve: Prepare Condiments; set aside. Place lahmejun pairs side by side on baking sheets. Bake, uncovered, in a 500° oven until hot (about 6 minutes). Carefully separate, garnish with mint leaves, and offer with condiments. Makes about 6 servings.

Condiments. Choose from the following: At least 10 stalks **celery**, with tops; 1 to 1½ cups **salt-cured olives;** 2 large **cucumbers,** thinly sliced; about 1 pound **pear-shaped tomatoes,** cored and cut into wedges; at least 10 **green onions** (including tops); 1 large can (7 oz.) **whole green chiles;** about 1 cup mildly hot **pickled peppers;** 1 pound **string cheese,** torn into thin strings; and 1 pound **feta cheese,** crumbled.

Pictured on facing page

Grilled Garlic-Orange Chicken

When you've got a busy week coming up, plan on this grilled chicken, which goes together easily in several advance steps. Garlic, rosemary, and orange peel lend elegant flavor to a supremely practical dish.

Initial preparation: About 45 minutes, plus at least 1 hour for marinating

Storage time: Marinade: 2 days to 1 week; chicken: 1 day

Final preparation: About 1 hour

6 **cloves garlic, minced or pressed**
1 **cup olive oil or salad oil**
1 **tablespoon grated orange peel**
1 **teaspoon chopped fresh rosemary or ½ teaspoon dry rosemary**
6 **small frying chickens (2¾ to 3¼ lbs. *each*)**
1 **tablespoon *each* paprika and black pepper**
   Orange slices, cut into quarters
   Fresh rosemary sprigs (optional)

Make-ahead steps: In a small bowl, combine garlic, oil, orange peel, and chopped rosemary. Cover and let stand at room temperature for at least 2 days or for up to 1 week.

Rinse chickens and pat dry; remove giblets and save for another use. Split chickens in half,

Per serving: 741 calories, 75 g protein, .97 g carbohydrates, 46 g total fat, 242 mg cholesterol, 226 mg sodium

brush all over with garlic oil, and arrange in two 10- by 15-inch rimmed baking pans. Cover and let marinate for 1 hour or refrigerate for up to 1 day.

Sprinkle chickens with paprika and pepper. Place on a barbecue grill 6 inches above a solid bed of medium-hot coals and cook, turning as needed, until browned (about 30 minutes total). Watch carefully to avoid flare-ups. Return chickens to baking pans. Cover and refrigerate for up to 1 day.

To serve: Bake, uncovered, in a 350° oven until meat near thighbone is no longer pink when slashed (about 55 minutes). Garnish with orange pieces and, if desired, rosemary sprigs. Makes 12 servings.

When time is short, relax—and rely on Grilled Garlic-Orange Chicken (recipe on facing page). Marinated and barbecued in advance, the succulent entrée is accented with fresh rosemary.

Family-style Herb Chicken

Initial preparation: About 45 minutes
Storage time: 1 day
Final preparation: None

Per serving: 324 calories, 44 g protein, .06 g carbohydrates, 15 g total fat, 136 mg cholesterol, 169 mg sodium

Offer a platter of chicken breasts and drumsticks at the next family outing. For an easy picnic treat, cook the herb-coated chicken until well browned, refrigerate, and serve the next day.

- ¼ **cup butter or margarine, melted**
- 1 **teaspoon dry marjoram leaves**
- ½ **teaspoon *each* salt, pepper, and dry basil, dry sage, dry thyme, and dry oregano leaves**
- 8 **chicken drumsticks (2¼ to 2½ lbs. *total*)**
- 2 **large whole chicken breasts (about 3 lbs. *total*), split**

Make-ahead steps: Stir together butter, marjoram, salt, pepper, basil, sage, thyme, and oregano.

Rinse chicken and pat dry; coat pieces with seasoned butter.

Arrange drumsticks in a shallow 10- by 15-inch baking pan. Bake in a 400° oven for 10 minutes. Remove pan from oven and add breasts, skin sides up. Continue baking until chicken is well browned and meat near bone is no longer pink when slashed (25 to 30 more minutes). Cover and refrigerate for up to 1 day. Makes 6 to 8 servings.

Pictured on page 2

Broccoli- & Cheese-stuffed Chicken Breasts

Initial preparation: About 45 minutes
Storage time: 1 day in refrigerator; 1 month in freezer
Final preparation: About 20 minutes

Per serving chicken: 306 calories, 41 g protein, 5 g carbohydrates, 13 g total fat, 113 mg cholesterol, 215 mg sodium

Per teaspoon sauce: 1 calorie, .01 g protein, .31 g carbohydrates, 0 g total fat, 0 mg cholesterol, .86 mg sodium

Fresh color and flavor are the hallmarks of this easy entrée. A day ahead, stuff tender chicken breasts with broccoli, onion, and Swiss cheese. Then simply bake and serve.

- 2 **tablespoons butter or margarine**
- 1 **small onion, chopped**
- 2 **teaspoons dry tarragon**
- ¾ **pound broccoli**
- 2 **tablespoons water**
- 1½ **cups (6 oz.) shredded Swiss cheese**
- 6 **skinned and boned chicken breast halves (about 2 lbs. *total*),**
  Chive-Tarragon Sauce (recipe follows)

Make-ahead steps: In a 10- to 12-inch frying pan, melt butter over medium heat. Add onion and tarragon. Cook, stirring occasion-ally, until onion is soft (about 7 minutes).

Trim off and discard tough stems from broccoli. Trim off flowerets, coarsely chop, and set aside. Peel tender stems and chop; add to flowerets. Add broccoli and water to pan; cover. Cook, stirring occasionally, until broccoli is tender-crisp (about 5 minutes). Remove from heat and stir in 1 cup of the cheese; let cool.

Place each breast half between 2 sheets of plastic wrap. Pound with a smooth mallet until about ¼ inch thick.

In center of each breast half, mound equal amounts of the broccoli mixture. Roll chicken around filling to enclose. Set filled breasts, seam sides down, in a buttered 9- by 13-inch baking pan. Sprinkle with remaining cheese. Cover and refrigerate for up to 1 day. (Or freeze for up to 1 month. Thaw overnight in refrigerator; or defrost in a microwave following manufacturer's directions.)

To serve: Bake, uncovered, in a 450° oven until meat turns white and filling is hot in center when cut (15 to 18 minutes). Meanwhile, prepare Chive-Tarragon Sauce and set aside. Broil chicken 4 to 6 inches below heat until cheese is browned (about 2 minutes). Offer sauce in a separate bowl to add to individual servings. Makes 6 servings.

Chive-Tarragon Sauce. In a bowl, stir together ⅓ cup **seasoned rice vinegar** or ⅓ cup rice wine vinegar, ½ teaspoon **sugar,** 1 tablespoon minced **fresh or dry chives,** and ½ teaspoon **dry tarragon.** Makes about ⅓ cup.

Arroz con Pollo

This Hispanic favorite improves when its rice, tomatoes, chicken, and broth rest for a day.

- 2 tablespoons salad oil
- 2 large onions, chopped
- 1 clove garlic, minced or pressed
- 2 medium-size tomatoes, peeled and diced
- 3 cups long-grain white rice
- 3 tablespoons capers, drained
- 1 quart regular-strength chicken broth
- 2 whole chicken breasts (about 2 lbs. *total*), split
- ½ cup chopped fresh cilantro (coriander) leaves

Initial preparation: About 45 minutes
Storage time: 1 day
Final preparation: About 25 minutes

Per serving: 303 calories, 17 g protein, 41 g carbohydrates, 8 g total fat, 35 mg cholesterol, 423 mg sodium

Make-ahead steps: Heat oil in a 3- to 4-quart pan over medium-high heat. When oil is hot, add onions and garlic. Cook, stirring occasionally, until onions are soft (about 10 minutes). Stir in tomatoes, rice, capers, and broth.

Place chicken on rice mixture. Bring to a boil; reduce heat, cover, and simmer until chicken is no longer pink when slashed in thickest part (about 15 minutes). Remove chicken. Cover and continue to simmer until rice is tender to bite (10 to 15 more minutes).

When chicken is cool enough to handle, pull off and discard skin and bones; shred meat. Stir chicken and cilantro into rice mixture. Let cool; cover and refrigerate for up to 1 day.

To serve: Reheat, covered, over low heat until hot (about 25 minutes); add a little water, if necessary, to prevent sticking. Makes 10 to 12 servings.

Spicy Chicken Gumbo

This spicy Louisiana specialty can be made almost entirely 3 days ahead. Relax—and enjoy.

- ½ cup olive oil or salad oil
- 1 cup all-purpose flour
- 2 medium-size onions, chopped
- 2 medium-size green bell peppers, seeded and chopped
- 1½ cups chopped celery
- 1 cup chopped green onions (including tops)
- 3 cloves garlic, minced or pressed
- 2 teaspoons ground thyme
- 1 teaspoon pepper
- 1 quart water
- 3 cans (28 oz. *each*) tomatoes
- 4 pounds chicken drumsticks, skinned
- 4 or 5 small dried hot red chiles or ½ teaspoon ground red pepper (cayenne)
- 2 bay leaves

Initial preparation: About 1½ hours
Storage time: 3 days in refrigerator; 1 month in freezer
Final preparation: About 1 hour

Per serving: 474 calories, 26 g protein, 55 g carbohydrates, 16 g total fat, 97 mg cholesterol, 530 mg sodium

- ¾ pound andouille or Polish sausage
- 1 pound fresh okra, ends trimmed and cut into ½-inch slices; or 1 pound frozen sliced okra, thawed
- 1 pound shelled and deveined medium-size shrimp
- 2 tablespoons filé powder (optional)
- 12 to 16 cups hot cooked rice

Make-ahead steps: In an 8- to 10-quart pan, blend oil and flour. Cook over medium-high heat, stirring, until dark red-brown (about 12 minutes). Remove from heat; add onions, bell peppers, celery, green onions, garlic, thyme, and pepper. Cook over medium heat, stirring occasionally, until vegetables are soft (about 15 minutes).

Add water, tomatoes (break up with a spoon) and their liquid, chicken, chiles, and bay leaves.

Bring to a boil; reduce heat, cover, and simmer until chicken is no longer pink when slashed in thickest part (about 30 minutes).

Slice sausage diagonally ¼ inch thick; add to pan. Increase heat to medium and cook, uncovered, until sausage is hot (about 10 minutes). Let cool; cover and refrigerate for up to 3 days. (Or freeze for up to 1 month. Thaw overnight in refrigerator; or defrost in a microwave following manufacturer's directions.)

To serve: Reheat, covered, stirring often, over low heat until simmering (about 1 hour). Add okra and shrimp. Cook, uncovered, over medium heat until shrimp turn pink (about 4 minutes). Remove from heat and, if desired, stir in filé powder. Ladle into soup bowls over rice. Makes 12 to 16 servings.

Enjoy a fiesta of glorious flavor *mañana* after taking a little time today
to create chicken- and cheese-filled Enchiladas with Tomatillo Sauce
(recipe on facing page).

Pictured on facing page

Enchiladas with Tomatillo Sauce

Initial preparation: About 1 hour
Storage time: 1 day
Final preparation: About 45 minutes

Per serving: 944 calories, 53 g protein, 41 g carbohydrates, 64 g total fat, 158 mg cholesterol, 1,177 mg sodium

You can make both the tomatillo sauce and the enchiladas the day before serving.

        Chicken Filling (recipe follows)
        Salad oil
12   **corn tortillas (6- to 7-inch diameter)**
        Tomatillo Sauce (recipe follows)
2   **cups (8 oz.) shredded jack cheese**
2   **cups finely shredded lettuce**
½   **cup sour cream**
½   **lime, thinly sliced**
⅓   **cup fresh cilantro (coriander) leaves**

Make-ahead steps: Prepare Chicken Filling; set aside. Pour oil to a depth of ½ inch into a 6- to 8-inch frying pan over medium-high heat. When oil ripples as pan is tilted, add a tortilla and cook, turning once, just until it begins to brown (about 5 seconds per side).

Lift out and lay flat on paper towels; immediately spoon about ½ cup of the filling down center. Roll to enclose.

Lay tortilla, seam side down, in a 10- by 15-inch rimmed baking pan. Repeat for remaining tortillas and filling. Prepare Tomatillo Sauce. Cover and refrigerate enchiladas and sauce separately for up to 1 day.

To serve: Bake enchiladas, covered, in a 350° oven until hot (about 30 minutes). Uncover and top with cheese. Continue baking until cheese is melted (about 10 more minutes). For each serving, spoon about ¼ cup of the sauce onto a plate. Add 2 enchiladas. Garnish with lettuce, sour cream, lime, and cilantro. Makes 6 servings.

Chicken Filling. Mix 4 cups coarsely shredded cooked **chicken,** 2 cups (8 oz.) shredded **jack cheese,** 1 large can (7 oz.) **diced green chiles,** and 1½ teaspoons **dry oregano leaves.** Season to taste with **salt.**

Tomatillo Sauce. In a 3- to 4-quart pan, combine 2 medium-size **onions,** chopped, with 6 tablespoons **salad oil** over medium-high heat. Cook, stirring, until onion is soft (about 5 minutes).

Stir in 1 large can (7 oz.) **diced green chiles;** 2 cans (13 oz. *each*) **tomatillos,** drained; 1 cup **regular-strength chicken broth;** 3 tablespoons **lime juice;** 2 teaspoons *each* **dry oregano leaves** and **sugar;** and 1 teaspoon **ground cumin.** Reduce heat and simmer, uncovered, for 25 minutes. Season to taste with **salt.** Whirl mixture in a blender until smooth. Cover and refrigerate for up to 1 day; reheat over low heat.

Curry-Apple Turkey Loaf

Initial preparation: About 1½ hours
Storage time: 1 day in refrigerator; 2 weeks in freezer
Final preparation: None

Per serving: 388 calories, 31 g protein, 19 g carbohydrates, 21 g total fat, 161 mg cholesterol, 286 mg sodium

Spicy curry and sweet-tart apples balance mild ground turkey in this lean and moist meat loaf. Serve right from the refrigerator.

2   **tablespoons butter or margarine**
2   **tart green apples (such as Granny Smith), peeled, cored, and chopped**
1   **medium-size onion, chopped**
5   **teaspoons curry powder**
1   **tablespoon ground coriander**
¼   **cup minced parsley**

2   **pounds ground turkey**
1   **large egg**
⅔   **cup fine dry bread crumbs**
½   **cup milk**
      Salt and pepper

Make-ahead steps: In a 10- to 12-inch frying pan, melt butter over medium heat. Add apples and onion. Cook, stirring often, until onion is lightly browned (about 15 minutes). Add curry powder, coriander, and parsley; continue to cook, stirring, for 2 more minutes. Let cool.

In a bowl, mix onion mixture, turkey, egg, bread crumbs, and milk. Season to taste with salt and pepper. Pat mixture into a 5- by 9-inch loaf pan. Bake in a 350° oven until browned and no longer pink in center when cut (about 1 hour). Invert onto a platter. Let cool; cover and refrigerate for up to 1 day. (Or freeze for up to 2 weeks. Thaw overnight in refrigerator; or defrost in a microwave following manufacturer's directions.) Makes 6 servings.

Company Classics

Over the years, experienced hosts develop a collection of favorites for entertaining. Here are some that have been enjoyed by many generations of company and cooks. Basically fool-proof, Boeuf Bourguignon forgives extra oven waiting for late arrivals; Chicken Cacciatore allows stretching for unexpected guests. Best of all, all these dishes need little last-minute attention.

But don't save our main courses just for special occasions! These "oldies but goodies" are appreciated and deserved just as much by family as they are by friends. And as you add them to your never-fail repertoire, remember, all these delicious classics can be prepared in advance.

Boeuf Bourguignon

- 2 tablespoons olive oil or salad oil
- 1 large onion, thinly sliced
- 1½ pounds boneless lean beef, cut into 1-inch cubes
- 2 teaspoons *each* sugar and red wine vinegar
- ¾ cup *each* dry red wine and regular-strength beef broth
- ½ teaspoon pepper Glazed Onions (recipe follows)
- 1 tablespoon butter or margarine
- 1½ pounds mushrooms, sliced
- 1 tablespoon cornstarch blended with ¼ cup water

Make-ahead steps: Heat 1 tablespoon of the oil in a 10- to 12-inch frying pan over medium heat.

When oil is hot, add onion. Cook, stirring, until soft (about 10 minutes). Add beef and remaining 1 tablespoon oil. Cook, stirring, until juices have evaporated.

Stir in sugar and vinegar and cook until meat is browned (about 10 minutes). With a slotted spoon, transfer meat and onion to a 2-quart casserole.

Add wine, broth, and pepper to frying pan. Bring to a boil, scraping browned bits from bottom of pan; pour into casserole. Let cool; cover and refrigerate for up to 1 day.

To Serve: Bake, covered, in a 375° oven for about 50 minutes. Meanwhile, prepare Glazed Onions; set aside.

In a 10- to 12-inch frying pan, melt butter over medium-high heat. Add mushrooms and cook until juices have evaporated (about 5 minutes); add to casserole. Stir cornstarch mixture into casserole. Cover and continue baking for 20 more minutes. Garnish with onions. Makes 6 servings.

Glazed Onions. Peel ½ pound **small white boiling onions** and make crosswise cuts in stem ends. Place in a 2- to 3-quart pan with enough boiling water to cover. Cook over medium heat until tender when pierced (about 20 minutes); drain well. Return to pan, add 1 tablespoon **butter** or margarine, and cook until onions are glazed.

Per serving: 298 calories, 29 g protein, 14 g carbohydrates, 15 g total fat, 76 mg cholesterol, 216 mg sodium

Chicken Cacciatore

- ¼ cup all-purpose flour
- 1 teaspoon salt
- ¼ teaspoon pepper
  3- to 3½-pound frying chicken, cut into pieces
- 4 tablespoons butter or margarine
- ½ pound mushrooms, thinly sliced
- 1 medium-size onion, chopped
- 2 green bell peppers, seeded and chopped
- 2 cloves garlic, minced or pressed
- 2 tablespoons chopped parsley
- ½ cup *each* dry white wine and regular-strength chicken broth
- 1 can (6 oz.) tomato paste
- ¼ teaspoon *each* dry marjoram, dry oregano leaves, and dry thyme leaves
- 1 package (8 oz.) fusilli Grated Parmesan cheese

Make-ahead steps: In a bag, combine flour, salt, and pepper. Add chicken, a few pieces at a time, and shake to coat completely.

In a 10- to 12-inch frying pan, melt 3 tablespoons of the butter over medium heat. Add chicken and cook until well browned (about 15 minutes). With a slotted spoon, transfer to a shallow 3-quart casserole.

Pour off and discard all but 3 tablespoons of the pan juices. Add mushrooms, onion, bell peppers, and garlic. Cook, stirring occasionally, until onion is soft (about 10 minutes).

Add parsley, wine, broth, tomato paste, marjoram, oregano,

and thyme; bring to a boil over medium-high heat. Reduce heat, cover, and simmer for 10 minutes. Spoon sauce over chicken. Let cool; cover and refrigerate for up to 1 day.

To Serve: Bake, covered, in a 350° oven for 30 minutes; uncover and continue baking until meat near thighbone is no longer pink when slashed (about 15 more minutes).

Meanwhile, in a 6- to 8-quart pan, cook fusilli in boiling salted water, following package directions, until barely tender to bite; drain well. Toss with remaining 1 tablespoon butter.

Arrange chicken in center of a deep serving platter. Surround with pasta and spoon sauce over chicken. Offer cheese to add to individual servings. Makes 4 servings.

Per serving: 859 calories, 53 g protein, 64 g carbohydrates, 43 g total fat, 171 mg cholesterol, 1,259 mg sodium

White Stew of Veal, Pork, or Lamb

2 **pounds boneless veal stew meat, boneless pork stew meat (butt or loin end), or lamb stew meat (neck or shoulder), cut into 1½-inch chunks**

¼ **teaspoon dry thyme leaves**

5 **or 6 black peppercorns**

1 **clove garlic**

3 **or 4 parsley sprigs**

1 **bay leaf**

1 **medium-size onion, minced**

½ **cup dry white wine**

1 **can (14½ oz.) regular-strength chicken or beef broth**

12 **small onions (1½- to 2-inch diameter); optional**
   About 1 cup whipping cream
   Salt
   Lemon juice

Make-ahead steps: In a 3- to 4-quart pan, combine meat, thyme, peppercorns, garlic, parsley, bay leaf, and minced onion. Cover and cook, stirring occasionally, over medium heat for 30 minutes. Add wine and broth. Reduce heat and simmer gently until meat is very tender when pierced (about 1 hour), adding whole onions, if desired, after 30 minutes. With a slotted spoon, lift out meat and whole onions and set aside. If desired, discard peppercorns, garlic, parsley, and bay leaf.

Add 1 cup of the cream to pan and bring to a boil over high heat. Cook, stirring occasionally, until sauce is thickened (7 to 10 minutes). Return meat, onions, and any juices to sauce. Cover and refrigerate for up to 2 days.

To Serve: Reheat, stirring occasionally, over medium heat until hot (about 25 minutes), adding a little cream if needed. Season to taste with salt and lemon juice. Makes 6 servings.

Per serving: 395 calories, 31 g protein, 3 g carbohydrates, 28 g total fat, 152 mg cholesterol, 421 mg sodium

Sole Florentine au Gratin

2 **pounds sole fillets**

½ **cup dry Madeira or dry sherry**

2 **tablespoons lemon juice**
   About ½ cup regular-strength chicken broth

2 **tablespoons butter or margarine**

2 **tablespoons all-purpose flour**

½ **teaspoon Dijon mustard**

⅓ **cup whipping cream**

¾ **cup shredded Swiss cheese**

2 **packages (10 oz. each) frozen chopped spinach, thawed**

Make-ahead steps: Rinse fish and pat dry. Fold fillets in half crosswise and arrange side by side in a 9- by 13-inch baking pan. Mix Madeira and lemon juice; pour over fish. Cover tightly and bake in a 400° oven until fish is just slightly translucent or wet inside when cut in thickest part (about 10 minutes).

Remove from oven; holding fish in pan with a wide spatula, drain off liquid into a measuring cup. Add enough of the chicken broth to make 1 cup liquid; set aside. Cover fish.

In a 1-quart pan, melt butter over medium heat. Stir in flour and mustard; cook until bubbly. Using a wire whisk, gradually add reserved 1 cup poaching liquid and cream. Cook, stirring, until bubbly and thickened (8 to 10 minutes). Stir in ½ cup of the cheese.

Squeeze moisture from spinach and distribute evenly in a shallow 1½-quart casserole; arrange fish evenly on top (do not unfold). Cover and refrigerate fish and sauce separately for up to 1 day.

To Serve: Reheat sauce, stirring occasionally, over medium heat until bubbly. Spoon evenly over fish; sprinkle with remaining ¼ cup cheese. Bake in a 450° oven until slightly bubbly (15 to 18 minutes). If necessary, broil 4 to 6 inches below heat until browned. Makes 6 servings.

Per serving: 309 calories, 36 g protein, 10 g carbohydrates, 14 g total fat, 111 mg cholesterol, 372 mg sodium

Pictured on facing page

Cool Salmon Steaks & Vegetables

Initial preparation: *About 1 hour*
Storage time: *1 day*
Final preparation: *About 5 minutes*

Per serving salmon and vegetables: 372 calories, 38 g protein, 29 g carbohydrates, 11 g total fat, 94 mg cholesterol, 93 mg sodium

Per tablespoon sauce: 5 calories, .39 g protein, .67 g carbohydrates, .11 g total fat, .42 mg cholesterol, 20 mg sodium

Bright colors, fresh flavors, and few calories—these are what recommend this entrée. Add the advantage of convenience.

- **1 pound green beans, ends trimmed**
- **4 salmon steaks (6 to 8 oz. *each*)**
- **8 to 12 red thin-skinned potatoes**
- **4 butter lettuce leaves, washed and crisped**
- **1½ cups cherry tomatoes**
  Radish Tartar Sauce (recipe follows)
  Dill sprigs (optional)
  Lemon wedges

Make-ahead steps: In a 5- to 6-quart pan, bring 3 quarts water to a boil over high heat. Add beans; cook, uncovered, just until bright green and barely tender (about 5 minutes). With tongs, lift out beans and immerse in ice water until cool.

Return water to boiling; add fish. Cover pan tightly and remove from heat. Let stand until fish is opaque throughout when cut (10 to 14 minutes). Lift out and immerse in ice water until cool.

Return water to boiling; add potatoes. Reduce heat, cover, and simmer until tender when pierced (20 to 25 minutes). Drain and immerse in ice water until cool.

Drain beans, fish, and potatoes. Arrange lettuce leaves on a platter and lay salmon steaks on top. Place beans, potatoes, and tomatoes around fish, grouping each separately. Let cool; cover and refrigerate for up to 1 day.

To Serve: Prepare Radish Tartar Sauce. Garnish fish with dill sprigs, if desired. Offer tartar sauce and lemon to add to individual servings. Makes 4 servings.

Radish Tartar Sauce. Mix 1 cup **plain yogurt** or sour cream, ¾ cup chopped **red radishes,** ⅓ cup minced **green onions** (including tops), 2 tablespoons drained **capers,** and 1 tablespoon **prepared horseradish** until blended. Season to taste with **salt.** Makes about 2 cups.

Faux Salmon Terrine

Initial preparation: *About 40 minutes*
Storage time: *1 day*
Final preparation: *About 5 minutes*

Per serving fish: 141 calories, 19 g protein, 4 g carbohydrates, 6 g total fat, 89 mg cholesterol, 194 mg sodium

Per tablespoon sauce: 100 calories, .15 g protein, .52 g carbohydrates, 11 g total fat, 8 mg cholesterol, 97 mg sodium

This cool fish mold is a trompe l'oeil; tomato paste tints the white fish with tempting salmon color.

- **1¾ pounds skinless firm, white-fleshed fish fillets (such as halibut or rockfish), cut into chunks**
- **2 large eggs**
- **1 can (6 oz.) tomato paste**
- **⅓ cup whipping cream**
- **5 teaspoons drained green peppercorns**
  Lemon Sauce (recipe follows)

Make-ahead steps: In a food processor, combine fish, eggs, tomato paste, and cream; whirl until smoothly puréed. Stir in peppercorns. Spoon into a deep, straight-sided 1-quart terrine or 4½- by 8½-inch loaf pan.

Cover terrine and set in a larger pan; place in a 350° oven. Pour boiling water to a depth of 1 inch into larger pan. Bake until fish mixture feels firm when lightly pressed in center (about 30 minutes). Lift from pan, uncover, and let cool. Cover and refrigerate for up to 1 day.

To Serve: Prepare Lemon Sauce. Cut terrine into ½-inch-thick slices; lift out with a wide spatula. Offer sauce to add to individual servings. Makes 8 to 10 servings.

Lemon Sauce. In a bowl, combine 1 cup **mayonnaise,** 1 tablespoon *each* **lemon juice** and chopped **parsley,** and 2 teaspoons **Dijon mustard.** Mix until well blended. Makes about 1 cup.

Hot and humid weather calls for cool and carefree meals. The fish, beans, and potatoes can all be prepared in advance for Cool Salmon Steaks & Vegetables (recipe on facing page).

Oven-poached Monkfish

Initial preparation: *About 45 minutes*
Storage time: *1 day*
Final preparation: *About 25 minutes*

Per serving: 522 calories, 39 g protein, 7 g carbohydrates, 38 g total fat, 144 mg cholesterol, 379 mg sodium

Most people assume that fish demands last-minute cooking— and often it does. But this elegant entrée poaches in advance.

- 1½ **pounds monkfish fillets**
  About ½ cup dry white wine or regular-strength chicken broth
- ½ **cup (¼ lb.) butter or margarine**
- ½ **pound mushrooms, sliced**
- ⅛ **teaspoon ground nutmeg**
- 2 **tablespoons all-purpose flour**
  Salt
- 1½ **cups (6 oz.) shredded Swiss cheese**
  Chopped parsley

Make-ahead steps: Remove membrane from fish and discard. Rinse fish and pat dry. Fold narrow ends under to make evenly thick pieces. Place in a shallow 1-quart baking pan; add ½ cup of the wine and cover with foil. Bake in a 400° oven until fish is just slightly translucent or wet inside when cut in thickest part (about 20 minutes). Pour off and reserve liquid; set aside.

In a 10- to 12-inch frying pan, melt ¼ cup of the butter over medium-high heat. Add mushrooms and nutmeg. Cook, stirring, until liquid has evaporated (about 3 minutes). Remove mushrooms and set aside.

In same pan, melt remaining ¼ cup butter over medium-high heat; stir in flour and cook until bubbly. Remove from heat and gradually add 1 cup of the poaching liquid (add more wine if needed). Return to heat and bring to a boil, stirring. Season to taste with salt. Cover and refrigerate fish, mushrooms, and sauce separately for up to 1 day.

To Serve: Drain any liquid from chilled fish. Spoon sauce evenly over fish; then top with cheese and mushrooms. Bake, uncovered, in a 400° oven until hot (about 20 minutes). Garnish with parsley. Makes 4 servings.

Fish Stew with Spicy Hot Mayonnaise

Initial preparation: *About 35 minutes*
Storage time: *Broth: 1 day; mayonnaise: 1 day*
Final preparation: *About 15 minutes*

Per serving stew: 222 calories, 30 g protein, 7 g carbohydrates, 8 g total fat, 53 mg cholesterol, 553 mg sodium

Per tablespoon mayonnaise: 107 calories, .20 g protein, .70 g carbohydrates, 12 g total fat, 9 mg cholesterol, 138 mg sodium

Prepare both broth and peppery mayonnaise a day in advance; simmer the fish just before serving.

- **Spicy Hot Mayonnaise (recipe follows)**
- 2 **tablespoons salad oil**
- 1 **large onion, chopped**
- 1 **large green bell pepper, seeded and chopped**
- 2 **cloves garlic, minced or pressed**
- 1 **can (16 oz.) pear-shaped tomatoes**
- 1½ **cups regular-strength chicken broth**
- ½ **cup dry white wine**
- 1 **bottle (8 oz.) clam juice**
- ¼ **teaspoon** *each* **dry basil, oregano, and thyme leaves**
- 2 **pounds boneless lean, mild-flavored fish fillets (such as rockfish or cod)**
  Salt and pepper
  Chopped parsley

Make-ahead steps: Prepare Spicy Hot Mayonnaise.

Heat oil in a 12- to 14-inch frying pan or 5-quart pan over medium-high heat. When oil is hot, add onion, bell pepper, and garlic; cook until vegetables are soft (about 10 minutes). Stir in tomatoes (break up with a spoon) and their liquid, broth, wine, clam juice, basil, oregano, and thyme. Bring to a boil; reduce heat, cover, and simmer for 15 minutes. Let cool; cover and refrigerate for up to 1 day.

To Serve: Cut fish into 1-inch cubes. Bring broth mixture to a boil. Add fish; reduce heat, cover, and simmer until fish is just slightly translucent or wet inside when cut (about 6 minutes). Season to taste with salt and pepper. Sprinkle with parsley. Offer with mayonnaise. Makes 4 to 6 servings.

Spicy Hot Mayonnaise. Stir ⅔ cup **mayonnaise,** 2 cloves **garlic,** minced or pressed, ¾ teaspoon **ground red pepper** (cayenne), 1 tablespoon **white wine vinegar,** and ¼ teaspoon **salt** until blended. Cover and refrigerate for up to 1 day.

Creamy Scallop Lasagne

Initial preparation: About 1 hour
Storage time: 1 day
Final preparation: About 1 hour and 55 minutes

Per serving: 666 calories, 43 g protein, 44 g carbohydrates, 35 g total fat, 156 mg cholesterol, 629 mg sodium

A creamy white wine sauce bathes scallops in this delicate seafood version of lasagne.

- **2 pounds bay or sea scallops**
  About ⅓ cup butter or margarine
- **1 cup chopped green onions (including tops)**
- **1 clove garlic, minced or pressed**
- **½ teaspoon fresh thyme or dry thyme leaves**
- **⅓ cup all-purpose flour**
- **1 cup *each* regular-strength chicken broth and whipping cream**
- **½ cup dry vermouth or dry white wine**
- **½ package (½ lb.) lasagne noodles**
- **2 cups (8 oz.) shredded Swiss cheese**

Make-ahead steps: Rinse scallops; drain. If using sea scallops, cut into ½-inch pieces. In a wide frying pan, melt 1 tablespoon of the butter over medium heat. Add green onions, garlic, and thyme; increase heat to medium-high and cook, stirring, for 1 minute. Add scallops and continue to cook, stirring, until opaque when cut (2 to 3 more minutes). Strain over a bowl; set aside scallops and juices.

In same pan, melt remaining butter. Add flour and cook, stirring, until golden. Remove from heat and mix in broth, cream, and vermouth. Bring to a boil over high heat, stirring. Remove from heat.

In a small pan, boil scallop juices over high heat, stirring, until reduced to 2 tablespoons. Add to sauce.

In a 6- to 8-quart pan, cook noodles in boiling salted water, following package directions, until barely tender to bite; drain. In a buttered 9- by 12-inch baking pan, layer a third each of the noodles, sauce, scallops, and cheese. Repeat 2 more times. Cover and refrigerate for up to 1 day.

To Serve: Bring to room temperature. Bake, covered, in a 350° oven for 20 minutes. Uncover and bake until golden (about 20 more minutes). Let stand for 15 minutes. Makes 6 servings.

Crêpe Shrimp Stack

Initial preparation: About 45 minutes
Storage time: Crêpes: 2 days; shrimp stack: 1 day
Final preparation: About 30 minutes

Per serving: 633 calories, 39 g protein, 16 g carbohydrates, 46 g total fat, 375 mg cholesterol, 728 mg sodium

Crêpes, shrimp, and cheese bake together in this impressive and convenient brunch entrée.

- **8 Crêpes (recipe follows)**
  About 1 cup (7 oz.) creamy garlic-herb cheese, at room temperature
- **½ pound small cooked shrimp**
- **3 tablespoons thinly sliced chives or green onions (including tops)**
- **2½ cups (10 oz.) shredded jack cheese**

Make-ahead steps: Prepare Crêpes. Spread about 2 tablespoons of the herb cheese on a crêpe. Place, cheese side up, on a 9-inch ovenproof plate. Mix shrimp, chives, and 2¼ cups of the jack cheese. Sprinkle ½ cup of the mixture over crêpe. Repeat layers, ending with a crêpe. Sprinkle with remaining ¼ cup jack cheese. Cover and refrigerate for up to 1 day.

To Serve: Bake, uncovered, in a 350° oven until hot (about 30 minutes). Makes 4 servings.

Crêpes. In a blender or food processor, whirl 2 **eggs** and ½ cup **all-purpose flour** until smooth. Add ⅔ cup **milk.**

Set a 6- to 7-inch crêpe pan or other flat-bottomed frying pan over medium heat until a drop of water dances in pan. Coat with ¼ teaspoon **butter** or margarine. Add ¼ cup of the batter, tilting pan to cover bottom. Cook crêpe until bottom is lightly browned (30 to 40 seconds). Turn and cook until other side is browned. Repeat with remaining batter, stirring occasionally; add butter to pan as needed.

Let cool; cover and refrigerate for up to 2 days. Bring to room temperature before using. Makes 8 crêpes.

Perfect for a patio picnic, Layered Mustard Shrimp (recipe on facing page) offers multidimensional taste appeal. The chilled mustard-flavored shrimp are spooned over lemon-seasoned noodles layered over crisp salad greens.

Pictured on facing page

Layered Mustard Shrimp

Initial preparation: *About 30 minutes*
Storage time: *1 day*
Final preparation: *About 5 minutes*

Per serving: 709 calories, 53 g protein, 78 g carbohydrates, 21 g total fat, 290 mg cholesterol, 1,643 mg sodium

Crisp greens topped with lemon-seasoned buckwheat noodles and mustard-sharpened cold shrimp add up to a midsummer night's feast for two. Double the tiered salad if the party expands.

Lemon Noodles (recipe follows)
2 tablespoons **butter** or **salad oil**
2 cloves **garlic,** minced or pressed
¼ cup finely chopped **onion**
⅛ teaspoon **ground red pepper (cayenne)**
¾ pound **shelled and deveined large shrimp** (30 to 35 per lb.)
¼ cup *each* **dry sherry** and **white wine vinegar**
1 tablespoon **Dijon mustard**
1 tablespoon finely chopped **fresh tarragon leaves** or 1 teaspoon **dry tarragon**
1 quart chilled **salad greens**

Make-ahead steps: Prepare Lemon Noodles.

In a 10- to 12-inch frying pan, melt butter over medium heat. Add garlic, onion, and ground red pepper; cook, stirring often, until onion is golden (about 5 minutes). Add shrimp and cook, stirring, until opaque when cut (4 to 5 minutes). Stir in sherry, vinegar, mustard, and tarragon; bring to a boil. Let cool; cover and refrigerate for up to 1 day.

To serve: Arrange salad greens on 2 dinner plates. Top with noodles and shrimp. Makes 2 servings.

Lemon Noodles. In a 5- to 6-quart pan, bring 4 quarts **water** to a boil over high heat. Add 6 ounces thin **buckwheat noodles** or vermicelli. Cook, stirring occasionally, until tender to bite (about 10 minutes).

Meanwhile, in a large bowl, stir together ¼ cup **lemon juice,** 2 tablespoons **soy sauce,** 2 teaspoons *each* **sesame oil** and finely chopped **fresh ginger,** and 1 teaspoon **sugar.**

Drain noodles; rinse with cold water until cool (about 2 minutes). Drain; mix with lemon juice mixture. Cover and refrigerate for up to 1 day.

Calamari Salad al Pesto

Initial preparation: *About 20 minutes*
Storage time: *1 day*
Final preparation: *None*

Per serving: 292 calories, 14 g protein, 9 g carbohydrates, 23 g total fat, 176 mg cholesterol, 44 mg sodium

Cold strips of squid combine with bright red bell pepper in a fresh basil dressing for this appetizing do-ahead salad.

Pesto (recipe follows)
¼ cup **olive oil**
1 small **onion,** finely diced
2 cloves **garlic,** minced or pressed
3 tablespoons chopped **walnuts**
1 pound **tenderized giant squid (calamari) steaks,** cut into ¼-inch-wide strips
2 tablespoons **dry sherry**
1 medium-size **red bell pepper,** seeded and diced
¼ cup *each* diced **celery** and **cider vinegar**
1 tablespoon chopped **parsley**
1 tablespoon **lemon** or **lime juice**
Salt and pepper
About 4 cups shredded **iceberg lettuce**

Make-ahead steps: Prepare Pesto; set aside.

Heat oil in a 10- to 12-inch frying pan over medium heat. When oil is hot, add onion, garlic, and nuts. Cook, stirring, until onion is soft and nuts are toasted (about 5 minutes). Add squid and sherry. Continue to cook, stirring, just until squid is opaque (about 1 more minute). With a slotted spoon, transfer mixture to a bowl.

Stir in bell pepper, celery, vinegar, parsley, lemon juice, and Pesto. Season to taste with salt and pepper. Cover and refrigerate for up to 1 day. Serve over lettuce. Makes 4 to 6 servings.

Pesto. In a blender or food processor, combine ¼ cup **olive oil,** ¼ cup lightly packed **fresh basil leaves,** 2 tablespoons **pine nuts,** 1 clove **garlic,** and, if desired, 1 teaspoon **dry white wine.** Whirl until smooth.

Layered Niçoise Salad

Initial preparation: About 1 hour
Storage time: 1 day
Final preparation: None

Per serving: 489 calories, 20 g protein, 24 g carbohydrates, 35 g total fat, 187 mg cholesterol, 575 mg sodium

Take your time to build this tiered summertime salad—you have up to a day before serving.

1½ **pounds small thin-skinned potatoes (½-inch diameter)**
 Anchovy Dressing (recipe follows)
 Salt and pepper
1 **pound green beans, ends removed, cut into 1-inch pieces**
¼ **cup *each* mayonnaise and sour cream**
1 **large can (12½ oz.) chunk-style tuna, drained**
5 **hard-cooked eggs, thinly sliced**
2 **quarts lightly packed butter lettuce leaves, torn into bite-size pieces**

Make-ahead steps: Place a rack in a 5- to 6-quart pan; pour in water to a depth of 1 to 1½ inches (water should not touch bottom of rack). Bring water to a boil over high heat; place potatoes on rack. Reduce heat to medium or medium-high, cover, and cook until potatoes are tender when pierced (about 20 minutes); add boiling water as needed to maintain water level. Remove potatoes from pan and let stand just until cool enough to touch.

Meanwhile, prepare Anchovy Dressing. Cut potatoes into ¼-inch slices and place in a deep 4- to 5-quart salad bowl. Add dressing and season to taste with salt and pepper. Let stand until cooled to room temperature.

In same pan, place beans on rack. Cover and steam over boiling water until bright green and tender to bite (about 10 minutes).

At once, immerse in ice water until cool; drain and pat dry.

Add mayonnaise and sour cream to potatoes; mix lightly. Layer beans over potatoes. Break tuna into pieces and distribute over beans; top with layers of eggs and lettuce. Cover and refrigerate for up to 1 day. Just before serving, mix lightly. Makes 6 to 8 servings.

Anchovy Dressing. In a bowl, combine ¾ cup **salad oil;** ½ cup *each* finely chopped **parsley** and **lemon juice;** 1 small **red onion,** finely chopped; ¼ cup **Dijon mustard;** 1 tablespoon drained **capers;** 4 canned **anchovy fillets,** minced; 1 large clove **garlic,** minced or pressed; and ¼ teaspoon **dill weed.** Stir until well blended.

Chard, Feta & Fila Pie

Initial preparation: About 45 minutes
Storage time: 1 day in refrigerator; 2 months in freezer
Final preparation: About 45 minutes

Per serving: 377 calories, 17 g protein, 21 g carbohydrates, 26 g total fat, 259 mg cholesterol, 1,101 mg sodium

Buttery layers of fila form a flaky topping over this hearty Swiss chard and feta cheese pie.

2 **pounds Swiss chard**
5 **tablespoons butter or margarine**
1 **large onion, thinly sliced**
4 **large eggs**
1½ **teaspoons *each* dry basil and dry oregano leaves**
¼ **teaspoon pepper**
2 **cups (about ¾ lb.) crumbled feta cheese**
4 **sheets fila dough (12 by 17 inches)**
2 **teaspoons fennel seeds**

Make-ahead steps: Fill a 5- to 6-quart pan three-quarters full of water and bring to a boil over high heat. Adding about a third of the chard leaves at a time, cook, uncovered, until stems are soft (about 3 minutes). As leaves are cooked, lift from pan with a slotted spoon and drain. Let cool; then coarsely chop.

In a 10- to 12-inch frying pan, melt 2 tablespoons of the butter over medium heat; add onion and cook, stirring occasionally, until soft (about 10 minutes).

In a bowl, lightly beat eggs to blend. Stir in chard, onion, basil, oregano, pepper, and cheese. Spread mixture evenly in an 8- by 12-inch baking pan or shallow 2-quart casserole.

Stack sheets of fila; fold once so width is same as or slightly larger than width of pan. Set pan on fila and trim to fit; discard trimmings.

In a small pan, melt remaining 3 tablespoons butter over medium heat. Lay a sheet of fila on chard mixture; brush with butter.

Continued on next page

...Chard, Feta & Fila Pie *continued*

Repeat layers of fila, brushing each sheet, including top, with butter.

With a sharp knife, cut through fila to make about 6 equal diamond-shaped sections. Cover and refrigerate for up to 1 day. (Or freeze for up to 2 months. Thaw overnight in refrigerator; or defrost in a microwave following manufacturer's directions.)

To Serve: Bake, uncovered, in a 375° oven until fila is well browned (40 to 45 minutes). Sprinkle with fennel. Makes 6 servings.

Poached Eggs & Prosciutto

Initial preparation: About 25 minutes
Storage time: 1 day
Final preparation: About 15 minutes

Per serving: 396 calories, 12 g protein, 10 g carbohydrates, 35 g total fat, 315 mg cholesterol, 382 mg sodium

Perfectly poached eggs nestle in prosciutto-lined tomatoes, topped with basil mayonnaise.

- **Cold Poached Eggs (recipe follows)**
- **Basil Mayonnaise (recipe follows)**
- **8 large tomatoes**
- **16 paper-thin slices prosciutto (about ¼ lb.)**

Make-ahead steps: Prepare Cold Poached Eggs and Basil Mayonnaise.

Fill a 1½- to 2-quart pan with water and bring to a boil over high heat. Immerse tomatoes, one at a time, for 5 to 10 seconds; lift out and peel. Slice off top quarter of each tomato. Scoop out center and let drain. Cover and refrigerate for up to 1 day.

To Serve: Place tomatoes on a serving platter and drape 2 slices of the prosciutto in each. Gently slip 1 egg into each tomato and top each with mayonnaise. Makes 8 servings.

Cold Poached Eggs. Pour water to a depth of 1½ inches into a buttered 12- to 14-inch frying pan. Heat until bubbles form on pan bottom. Add 1 tablespoon **white vinegar** or cider vinegar. Break 8 **eggs,** one at a time, into water. With water barely simmering, cook until done to your liking (for soft yolks and firm whites, allow 3 to 5 minutes).

With a slotted spoon, lift eggs from water. Place immediately in ice water to stop cooking. Cover and refrigerate for up to 1 day. Drain before using.

Basil Mayonnaise. In a blender or food processor, combine 1 **egg,** 2 tablespoons **lemon juice,** ½ teaspoon **dry mustard,** and 1 cup packed **fresh basil leaves.** Whirl until smoothly puréed. With motor running, gradually add 1 cup **salad oil.** Season to taste with more lemon juice. Cover and refrigerate for up to 1 day.

Vegetable Frittata Loaf

Initial preparation: About 1 hour
Storage time: 1 day
Final preparation: About 1 hour

Per serving: 496 calories, 21 g protein, 35 g carbohydrates, 30 g total fat, 341 mg cholesterol, 926 mg sodium

Astonish your guests with our spectacular sandwich. Make it hours before the party starts.

- **1 round loaf (1 lb.) French bread (about 12 inches wide)**
- **⅓ cup olive oil**
- **¾ pound mild Italian sausages, casings removed**
- **1 small onion, chopped**
- **2 cloves garlic, minced or pressed**
- **2 small zucchini, thinly sliced**
- **1 large tomato, cored, peeled, seeded, and chopped**
- **¼ cup chopped fresh basil leaves**
- **9 eggs**
- **½ teaspoon *each* salt and pepper**
- **½ cup grated Parmesan cheese**

Make-ahead steps: Cut bread in half horizontally. Hollow out halves, leaving ½-inch-thick shells. Brush inside with 3 tablespoons of the oil. Reassemble loaf, wrap in foil, and warm in a 350° oven for 10 minutes.

Continued on next page

Crumble sausages into a 9- or 10-inch frying pan (preferably with a nonstick coating) and cook, stirring, over medium heat until browned (about 10 minutes). Discard all but 2 tablespoons of the drippings. Set meat aside. Add onion and garlic to pan; cook, stirring occasionally, until onion is soft (about 10 minutes). Add zucchini and tomato; cook, stirring, until liquid has evaporated. Add basil; remove from heat.

In a large bowl, beat eggs with salt and pepper. Stir in vegetables and sausages.

Wipe pan clean. Heat 1 more tablespoon of the oil over medium heat; when oil is hot, pour in egg mixture. As eggs set on bottom, lift cooked portion with a spatula to allow uncooked egg to flow underneath. When eggs are set and browned on bottom, invert a plate over frittata. Flip frittata onto plate. Return pan to heat and add remaining oil; slide frittata into pan and cook until other side is lightly browned. Sprinkle with cheese.

Unwrap loaf; lay hollow bottom half of bread over frittata. Invert frittata into bread. Set top half of bread in place. Wrap in foil and refrigerate for up to 1 day.

To Serve: Bake, wrapped, in a 300° oven until warm in center (about 1 hour). Makes 7 or 8 servings.

Pictured on facing page

Gruyère & Mushroom Tart

Initial preparation: About 1 hour
Storage time: Pastry: 1 hour to 1 day; tart: 1 day
Final preparation: About 10 minutes, plus 1 to 1½ hours for pastry to rise

Per serving: 792 calories, 28 g protein, 57 g carbohydrates, 51 g total fat, 212 mg cholesterol, 507 mg sodium

This savory cheese tart adapts well to a busy cook's schedule.

Rich Yeast Pastry (recipe follows)
1 **pound medium-size or large mushrooms**
2 **tablespoons butter or margarine**
½ **cup chopped onion**
2 **tablespoons chopped parsley**
2 **cups (8 oz.) firmly packed shredded Gruyère or Swiss cheese**
Salt and pepper

Make-ahead steps: Prepare Rich Yeast Pastry.

Remove stems from mushrooms; finely chop and set aside. Cut mushroom caps in half.

In a 10- to 12-inch frying pan, melt butter over medium-high heat. Add mushroom caps and cook, stirring, until liquid has evaporated and mushrooms are browned (8 to 10 minutes). With a slotted spoon, lift out mushroom caps and set aside.

Add chopped stems and onion to pan; cook, stirring often, until onion begins to brown (about 8 minutes). Mix in 1 tablespoon of the parsley.

Divide pastry into 4 equal pieces; keep remainder cold as you shape each piece.

Shape 1 piece of dough into a ball; flatten and roll out on a lightly floured board into a 7- to 8-inch round. Lay pastry at one end of a greased 10- by 15-inch baking pan. Fold ½ inch of the edge over onto pastry; flute or crimp edge to form a shallow rim.

Repeat for another round of dough and place at other end of pan. Sprinkle each pastry with ¼ cup of the cheese; top with a quarter *each* of the mushroom caps and onion mixture. Shape remaining dough, place on another pan, and fill.

Cover pans with plastic wrap and refrigerate for up to 1 day.

To Serve: Set covered pans in a warm place and let pastries rise until rims are nearly doubled (1 to 1½ hours). Bake in a 450° oven, 1 pan on lowest rack and 1 on a rack in upper third of oven, until pastry is well browned on bottom (5 to 7 minutes), switching pan positions halfway through baking.

Sprinkle with remaining 1 tablespoon parsley; season to taste with salt and pepper. Makes 4 main-dish tarts.

Rich Yeast Pastry. In a small pan, warm ½ cup **milk** to 110°F; remove from heat and sprinkle 1 package **active dry yeast** over milk. Let stand until softened.

Meanwhile, in a bowl, mix 2 cups **all-purpose flour** with 2 teaspoons **sugar.** Add ½ cup (¼ lb.) **butter** or margarine, cut into small pieces. Rub mixture with your fingers until it resembles coarse crumbs. Add yeast mixture and 1 large **egg yolk.** Stir just until dough is thoroughly moistened and holds together.

Pat dough into a ball and place in bowl. Cover with plastic wrap and refrigerate for at least 1 hour or for up to 1 day.

Gruyère & Mushroom Tart (recipe on facing page) goes together in three easy steps. First, prepare the tender yeast dough; later, form, fill, and chill the cheese-and-vegetable tart. Then just bake before serving.

Salads & Vegetables

Though salads and vegetables often play second fiddle to the main course, the make-ahead examples in this chapter deserve to share the spotlight with any entrée. Indeed, you'll enjoy several of these recipes as light entrées in their own right, served solo. For lunch, consider Antipasto Pasta Salad, with fresh artichokes tossed in a raspberry vinaigrette; Tropical Salad with Green Peppercorns, pineapple, and papaya; Tomato-smothered Leeks; or multilayered Summer Squash Gratin. Or ready to enhance any simply cooked meat, poultry, or fish are Zesty Black Bean Salad, tender Asparagus with Oranges, and Glazed Roasted Onions.

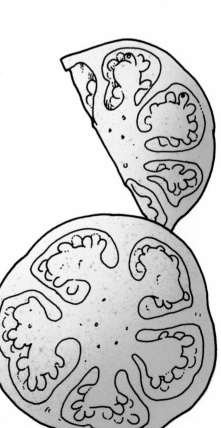

Antipasto Pasta Salad

Initial preparation: About 10 minutes
Storage time: 1 day
Final preparation: None

Per serving: 299 calories, 10 g protein, 18 g carbohydrates, 22 g total fat, 12 mg cholesterol, 410 mg sodium

The lively ingredients of an Italian appetizer—fresh vegetables, prosciutto, and Parmesan cheese—join pasta and a raspberry vinaigrette in this satisfying salad. It waits until you're ready to serve with crusty bread.

Raspberry Vinaigrette (recipe follows)

10 **cooked artichoke hearts or 1 can (8½ oz.) artichoke hearts in water, drained**
5 **cups cold cooked pasta twists**
1 **cup pitted ripe olives**
3 **cups cooked broccoli flowerets**
¼ **pound mushrooms, thinly sliced**
1 **cup quartered cherry tomatoes**
⅛ **pound prosciutto, cut into thin strips**
1 **cup (about 5 oz.) grated Parmesan cheese**

Make-ahead steps: Prepare Raspberry Vinaigrette; set aside.

Cut artichoke hearts in quarters. Mix with pasta, olives, broccoli, mushrooms, tomatoes, prosciutto, cheese, and vinaigrette. Cover and refrigerate for up to 1 day. Makes 8 to 10 servings.

Raspberry Vinaigrette. In a bowl, combine ½ cup **raspberry vinegar,** ⅔ cup **olive oil,** 1½ teaspoons **dry basil,** and ¼ teaspoon **pepper.** Mix until blended.

Avocado & Brown Rice Salad

Initial preparation: About 50 minutes
Storage time: Rice: 2 days; avocados: 1 day
Final preparation: About 5 minutes

Per serving: 292 calories, 4 g protein, 26 g carbohydrates, 20 g total fat, 4 mg cholesterol, 343 mg sodium

Silken avocados contrast deliciously with the sturdy flavor and texture of brown rice. To save last-minute fuss, prepare both well in advance, then just toss together when it's time to serve. This salad goes particularly well with grilled meats.

1 **tablespoon butter or margarine**
1 **cup long-grain brown rice**
2½ **cups regular-strength chicken broth**
1½ **teaspoons dry marjoram**
3 **medium avocados (about 2 lbs. *total*)**
½ **cup minced parsley**
3 **green onions, thinly sliced**
5 **tablespoons lemon juice**
3 **tablespoons olive oil or salad oil**
1 **teaspoon coarsely ground pepper**

Make-ahead steps: In a 10- to 12-inch frying pan, melt butter over medium-high heat. Add rice and cook, stirring occasionally, until rice turns opaque (about 3 minutes). Add broth and marjoram; bring to a boil over high heat. Reduce heat, cover, and simmer until rice is tender to bite (about 40 minutes). Let cool; cover and refrigerate for up to 2 days.

Cut 2 of the avocados in half, pit, and peel; cut into ½-inch cubes. In a large bowl, gently mix diced avocados with parsley, green onions, lemon juice, oil, and pepper. Cover and refrigerate for up to 1 day.

To serve: In a large bowl, mix rice with diced avocado mixture. Cut remaining avocado in half, pit, and peel. Cut each half lengthwise into thin slices and arrange, overlapping, over rice mixture. Serve cold or at room temperature. Makes 7 or 8 servings.

Green & Gold Salad (recipe on facing page) composes a symphony of color, texture, and taste. Elegant molded layers of celery, carrots, and cabbage are enhanced by a mustardy mayonnaise.

Minted Cabbage Slaw

Initial preparation: About 15 minutes
Storage time: 1 day
Final preparation: About 5 minutes

Per serving: 78 calories, 1 g protein, 7 g carbohydrates, 5 g total fat, 0 mg cholesterol, 20 mg sodium

As refreshing as it is easy to assemble, this crisp mint-seasoned slaw is a dependable crowd-pleaser at summertime picnics.

- **2 medium heads cabbage (about 2 lbs. *each*)**
- **⅓ cup olive oil or salad oil**
- **⅓ cup lemon juice**
- **3 tablespoons *each* white wine vinegar and water**
- **1 teaspoon *each* pepper and sugar**
- **1 large red onion**
- **1 cup chopped fresh mint or ½ cup dry mint leaves**

Make-ahead steps: Gently remove large outer cabbage leaves, rinse, and wrap in paper towels. Enclose in a plastic bag and refrigerate for up to 1 day.

Thinly shred cabbage heads; discard cabbage cores.

In a large bowl, mix oil, lemon juice, vinegar, water, pepper, and sugar. Add shredded cabbage.

Cut onion into 4 wedges; finely chop 3 of the wedges and add to cabbage along with mint; mix well. Cover with plastic wrap and refrigerate for up to 1 day. Seal remaining onion wedge in a plastic bag and refrigerate for up to 1 day.

To serve: Line a wide, shallow salad bowl with reserved cabbage leaves, arranging so edges are above rim. Fill bowl with chilled slaw. Thinly slice reserved onion wedge and scatter over slaw. Makes 12 to 14 servings.

Pictured on facing page

Green & Gold Salad

Initial preparation: About 40 minutes, plus 8 hours for chilling
Storage time: Mayonnaise: 1 week; salad: 2 days
Final preparation: About 2 minutes

Per serving salad: 57 calories, 2 g protein, 13 g carbohydrates, .19 g total fat, 0 mg cholesterol, 28 mg sodium

Per tablespoon mayonnaise: 80 calories, .13 g protein, .55 g carbohydrates, 9 g total fat, 6 mg cholesterol, 78 mg sodium

Layers of crisp raw vegetables compose this colorful salad. Celery, carrots, green onions, and bell pepper glisten with cabbage shreds in an apple-lemon gelatin. A mustardy lemon mayonnaise complements the cool salad.

- **Lemon Mayonnaise (recipe follows)**
- **2 envelopes unflavored gelatin**
- **3 cups apple juice**
- **½ cup lemon juice**
- **1 cup diced celery**
- **3½ cups shredded carrots (about 4 large)**
- **½ cup *each* chopped green onions and green bell pepper**
- **3 cups finely shredded cabbage**

Make-ahead steps: Prepare Lemon Mayonnaise.

In a 2- to 2½-quart pan, sprinkle gelatin over apple juice; let stand until soft (about 5 minutes). Place over low heat and stir until gelatin is dissolved. Remove from heat and stir in lemon juice.

Set pan in a large bowl filled with ice cubes. Stir until mixture reaches consistency of unbeaten egg whites (about 10 minutes).

Combine celery with ½ cup of the gelatin mixture; spoon into a lightly oiled 5- by 9-inch loaf pan. Mix carrots with 1½ cups of the remaining gelatin mixture; gently spoon carrot mixture over celery layer. Sprinkle with green onions and bell pepper.

Combine remaining gelatin with cabbage. Carefully spoon over onion layer; press surface lightly until level. Cover and refrigerate for at least 8 hours or for up to 2 days.

To serve: Unmold onto a plate and serve with Lemon Mayonnaise. Makes 12 servings.

Lemon Mayonnaise. Combine 1 cup **mayonnaise,** 2 teaspoons **Dijon mustard,** ¼ cup **lemon juice,** and ¼ teaspoon **pepper;** mix until smoothly blended. Cover and refrigerate for up to 1 week.

Pictured on front cover

Corn & Red Pepper Relish Salad

Initial preparation: About 10 minutes
Storage time: 1 week in refrigerator; 4 months in freezer
Final preparation: None

Per serving: 126 calories, 3 g protein, 31 g carbohydrates, .76 g total fat, 0 mg cholesterol, 9 mg sodium

Bright red pepper and yellow corn create a sunburst of color in this simple salad. Boil the dressing, add the vegetables, and season to taste. Wonderfully convenient, the salad waits for up to a week before serving.

- 1⅓ **cups distilled white vinegar**
- ½ **cup sugar**
- ½ **teaspoon *each* celery seeds and mustard seeds**
- ½ **cup minced onion**
- 2 **packages (10 oz. *each*) frozen corn kernels, thawed and drained**
- 1 **cup canned red peppers or canned pimentos, drained and thinly sliced**
  Salt and pepper
  Red leaf lettuce (optional)

Make-ahead steps: In a 2- to 3-quart pan, combine vinegar, sugar, celery seeds, mustard seeds, and onion. Bring to a boil over high heat. Reduce heat and simmer, uncovered, for 5 minutes. Remove from heat and stir in corn and red peppers; season to taste with salt and pepper. Let cool; cover and refrigerate for up to 1 week. (Or freeze for up to 4 months. Thaw overnight in refrigerator; or defrost in a microwave following manufacturer's directions.)

To serve: Drain or lift from dish with a slotted spoon. Serve on a bed of lettuce leaves, if desired. Makes 8 servings.

Zesty Black Bean Salad

Initial preparation: About 1¼ hours
Storage time: 1 day
Final preparation: Garnish

Per serving: 135 calories, 9 g protein, 21 g carbohydrates, 3 g total fat, 0 mg cholesterol, 1,007 mg sodium

Red bell pepper, yellow lemon peel, and green onions put visual excitement, as well as flavor, into this black bean salad. Long popular in Latin American cooking, mild but distinctively flavored black beans are now available in many supermarkets.

- 1¾ **cups (½ lb.) black beans, sorted of debris and rinsed**
- ½ **teaspoon ground red pepper (cayenne)**
- 2 **quarts regular-strength chicken broth or water**
- 1 **small red bell pepper, seeded and finely chopped**
- ½ **cup diagonally sliced green onions**
- 2 **tablespoons balsamic vinegar or red wine vinegar**
- 1 **tablespoon lemon juice**
- 1 **tablespoon very thinly slivered lemon peel (yellow part only)**
- ½ **cup firmly packed cilantro (coriander) sprigs, rinsed and drained**
  Salt

Make-ahead steps: In a 4- to 5-quart pan, combine beans, ¼ teaspoon of the ground red pepper, and broth. Bring to a boil over high heat. Reduce heat, cover, and simmer until beans are tender to bite (about 45 minutes). Pour beans into a strainer, discarding liquid. Rinse beans under cold water until water runs clear and beans are cool; bite to test (about 3 minutes). Drain well.

In a bowl, mix beans with bell pepper, green onions, vinegar, lemon juice, lemon peel, and remaining ¼ teaspoon ground red pepper. Set aside several cilantro sprigs. Chop remaining cilantro and stir into beans. Season to taste with salt. Cover and refrigerate for up to 1 day.

To serve: Garnish with cilantro sprigs. Makes 6 to 8 servings.

Pictured on page 34

Italian Garden Salad

Initial preparation: About 2 hours
Storage time: 2 days
Final preparation: None

Per serving: 258 calories, 5 g protein, 22 g carbohydrates, 20 g total fat, 0 mg cholesterol, 777 mg sodium

To allow the tomato, olives, capers, garlic, and other flavors to blend until mellow, make this Italian eggplant salad one or two days before you plan to serve it.

- 1 **eggplant (about 1 lb.)**
  About ⅓ cup olive oil
- 2 **large cloves garlic, minced or pressed**
- 1 **small onion, coarsely chopped**
- 2 **large stalks celery, cut into ½-inch pieces**
- 1 **can (15 oz.) tomato purée**
- 2 **tablespoons drained capers**
- ½ **cup pimento-stuffed green olives, sliced**
- ¼ **cup pine nuts**
- 2 **tablespoons red wine vinegar**
- 1 **tablespoon sugar**
- ½ **cup dry red wine**

Make-ahead steps: Cut off and discard ends of eggplant. Cut eggplant into 1-inch cubes. Brush a 12- by 15-inch rimmed baking pan with oil. Lay cubes in pan and brush with some of the remaining oil, reserving 2 tablespoons. Bake, uncovered, in a 400° oven until eggplant mashes very easily when pressed (about 40 minutes).

Heat remaining 2 tablespoons oil in a 5- to 6-quart pan over medium heat. When oil is hot, add garlic, onion, and celery. Cook, uncovered, stirring often, until celery is soft (about 25 minutes).

Add eggplant, tomato purée, capers, olives, pine nuts, vinegar, sugar, and wine. Cook, uncovered, stirring occasionally, until mixture is thick enough to flow back slowly when a spoon is pulled through it (30 to 40 more minutes). Let cool; cover and refrigerate for up to 2 days. Makes 4 or 5 servings.

Soy-braised Eggplant Salad

Initial preparation: About 45 minutes
Storage time: 1 day in refrigerator; 1 month in freezer
Final preparation: Garnish

Per serving: 140 calories, 2 g protein, 11 g carbohydrates, 10 g total fat, 0 mg cholesterol, 1,034 mg sodium

Hot and tart Hunan flavors characterize this Chinese eggplant salad. Simmer the eggplant in a seasoned soy sauce; garnish with cilantro, chiles, and more ginger before serving.

- 1 **medium-size eggplant (about 1 lb.)**
- 3 **to 6 tablespoons salad oil**
- 1 **cup water**
- ¼ **cup soy sauce**
- 6 **thin slices fresh ginger (*each* about the size of a quarter)**
- 2 **cloves garlic, minced or pressed**
- 1 **teaspoon sugar**
- 3 **tablespoons red wine vinegar**
- ⅓ **cup coarsely chopped fresh cilantro (coriander) leaves**
- 2 **teaspoons minced fresh ginger**
- ¼ **to ½ teaspoon crushed dried hot red chiles**

Make-ahead steps: Cut off and discard ends of eggplant. Cut eggplant lengthwise into 1-inch-thick wedges. Heat 3 tablespoons of the oil in a 12- to 14-inch frying pan over medium-high heat. When oil is hot, add eggplant, cut sides down. Cook, turning once, until lightly browned (about 5 minutes). Remove eggplant as it browns to make room for remaining pieces, adding more oil as needed. When all eggplant is browned, return to pan and add water, soy, ginger slices, garlic, and sugar.

Reduce heat, cover, and simmer, turning eggplant occasionally, until it mashes easily when pressed (25 to 30 minutes). Remove from heat. Add vinegar. Let cool; cover and refrigerate for up to 1 day. (Or freeze for up to 1 month. Thaw overnight in refrigerator; or defrost in a microwave following manufacturer's directions.)

To serve: Serve cold or at room temperature. Garnish with cilantro, minced ginger, and chiles. Makes 4 servings.

Sweet Onion Potato Salad

Initial preparation: *About 45 minutes*
Storage time: *1 day*
Final preparation: *None*

Per serving: 323 calories, 3 g protein, 28 g carbohydrates, 23 g total fat, 16 mg cholesterol, 329 mg sodium

Ready when you are, this make-ahead salad offers a sweet, mild onion flavor. Choose thin-skinned potatoes for their firm, waxy texture that holds up well in boiling. Leave the skins on for extra color, flavor, and texture—and less work!

- 3 **pounds medium-size red thin-skinned potatoes**
- 1 **large mild white or red onion**
- 1 **cup thinly sliced celery**
- 1 **large Golden Delicious apple, cored and diced**
- 12 **pimento-stuffed green olives, sliced**
- ⅓ **cup chopped sweet pickles**
- 1½ **cups mayonnaise**
- 1 **teaspoon Dijon mustard**
- 2 **tablespoons distilled white vinegar**
- 1 **teaspoon bottled steak sauce or soy sauce**
  Salt and pepper

Make-ahead steps: In a 4- to 5-quart pan, pour in water to a depth of 1 inch and add potatoes. Bring to a boil; then cover and cook over medium heat until tender when pierced (25 to 30 minutes). Drain well and let cool. Peel potatoes, if desired; then dice and place in a large bowl.

Cut onion into quarters and slice thinly; add to potatoes with celery, apple, olives, and pickles.

In a small bowl, stir together mayonnaise, mustard, vinegar, and steak sauce. Gently mix with potatoes. Season to taste with salt and pepper. Cover and refrigerate for up to 1 day. Makes 10 to 12 servings.

Tropical Salad with Green Peppercorns

Initial preparation: *About 15 minutes*
Storage time: *1 day*
Final preparation: *2 minutes*

Per serving: 127 calories, .99 g protein, 32 g carbohydrates, .76 g total fat, 0 mg cholesterol, 28 mg sodium

After a few minutes of preparation, this salad of pineapple, mint, and green peppercorns waits in the refrigerator as its refreshing flavors blend. Serve beside a fan of papaya. Garnish with strawberries and mint sprigs for a colorful presentation.

- 1 **medium-size ripe pineapple (about 4 lbs.)**
- 2 **teaspoons drained green peppercorns in brine**
- 2 **tablespoons honey**
- 2 **tablespoons orange-flavored liqueur or orange juice**
- 2 **tablespoons chopped fresh mint or 2 teaspoons dry mint leaves**
- 1 **medium-size papaya**
- 6 **large strawberries**
- 6 **mint sprigs**

Make-ahead steps: Peel and core pineapple. Dice into ¼- to ½-inch pieces and place in a bowl. Chop peppercorns and add to fruit with honey, orange liqueur, and chopped mint; mix gently. Cover and refrigerate for up to 1 day.

To serve: Peel, seed, and cut papaya into wedges. Garnish pineapple mixture with papaya, strawberries, and mint sprigs. Makes 6 servings.

Just one scoop of Sweet Onion Potato Salad (recipe on facing page) won't quite satisfy: you'll want at least two. Tossed with apple, celery, and olives, the salad is the perfect accompaniment to a sandwich made with Picnic Caper Loaf (recipe on page 27).

Pictured on page 71

Asparagus with Oranges

Initial preparation: *About 10 minutes*
Storage time: *1 day in refrigerator; 6 months in freezer*
Final preparation: *About 10 minutes*

Per serving: 53 calories, 2 g protein, 4 g carbohydrates, 4 g total fat, 10 mg cholesterol, 40 mg sodium

At your convenience, cook the asparagus ahead. When it's time to serve, just heat it in garlic butter that is then mixed with orange juice and reduced to create a sauce.

- 1½ **pounds asparagus, tough ends removed**
- 2 **tablespoons butter or olive oil**
- 1 **large clove garlic, minced or pressed**
- 1½ **teaspoons grated orange peel**
- ¼ **cup orange juice**
  Salt and pepper

Make-ahead steps: Pour water to a depth of 1 inch into a 12- to 14-inch frying pan and bring to a boil over high heat. Lay asparagus spears in pan and cook, uncovered, until stems are just tender when pierced (about 4 minutes); drain. Immediately immerse asparagus in cold water; drain. Cover and refrigerate for up to 1 day. (Or freeze for up to 6 months. Thaw overnight in refrigerator; or defrost in a microwave following manufacturer's directions.)

To serve: In a 12- to 14-inch frying pan, melt butter with garlic and orange peel over medium-high heat. When butter is melted, add asparagus. Cook over high heat, shaking pan to mix flavors, just until asparagus is hot (2 to 3 minutes). Lift out asparagus and place on a serving platter. Add orange juice to pan and bring to a boil. Cook until reduced to about 3 tablespoons. Pour over asparagus.

Season to taste with salt and pepper. Makes 6 servings.

High-desert Corn Casserole

Initial preparation: *About 30 minutes*
Storage time: *1 day*
Final preparation: *About 30 minutes*

Per serving: 213 calories, 11 g protein, 19 g carbohydrates, 12 g total fat, 87 mg cholesterol, 224 mg sodium

Fresh corn is the tantalizing basis of this casserole. Slice kernels from ears; purée half and sauté the remainder with jalapeño chiles and red bell peppers.

- 4 **or 5 large ears of corn, husked**
- 5 **fresh jalapeño or serrano chiles**
- 2 **tablespoons salad oil**
- 1 **medium-size onion, chopped**
- 1 **medium-size red bell pepper, seeded and finely chopped**
- 1 **cup small curd cottage cheese**
- 2 **large eggs**
- 1 **tablespoon cornstarch**
  Salt and pepper
- 1 **cup (4 oz.) shredded Cheddar cheese**

Make-ahead steps: Cut enough kernels from corn to make 4 cups. Set aside.

Seed and chop 3 of the chiles. Refrigerate remaining 2 chiles. Heat oil in a 10- to 12-inch frying pan over medium-high heat. When oil is hot, add chopped chiles, onion, and bell pepper; cook, stirring often, until onion is soft and bell pepper is tender to bite (about 10 minutes). Add 2 cups of the corn and stir until hot.

Meanwhile, in a food processor or blender; combine remaining 2 cups corn, cottage cheese, eggs, and cornstarch; whirl until smooth (about 2 minutes).

Remove cooked vegetables from heat and stir in puréed mixture. Season to taste with salt and pepper. Place in a shallow 10-inch round or oval baking pan. Sprinkle Cheddar cheese over vegetables. Cover and refrigerate for up to 1 day.

To serve: Uncover and bake in a 375° oven until mixture puffs in center and cheese begins to brown at edges (about 30 minutes). Garnish with remaining whole chiles. Makes 8 servings.

Minty Carrots & Wild Rice

Initial preparation: About 1 hour
Storage time: 1 day in refrigerator; 4 months in freezer
Final preparation: About 15 minutes; or garnish

Per serving: 138 calories, 3 g protein, 19 g carbohydrates, 6 g total fat, 16 mg cholesterol, 284 mg sodium

Sweet cooked carrots join wild rice and mint in this hearty and handy accompaniment to roast pork or turkey.

- ¼ cup butter or margarine
- ½ cup wild rice, rinsed and drained
- 1½ cups regular-strength chicken broth
- 2 pounds small slender carrots, peeled
- ½ cup finely chopped fresh mint leaves or 2 tablespoons dry mint, crumbled
- 3 tablespoons lemon juice
  Salt and pepper
  Mint or parsley sprigs

Make-ahead steps: In a 10- to 12-inch frying pan, melt butter over medium-high heat. Add rice and broth. Reduce heat, cover, and simmer for 35 minutes. Add carrots and continue to cook until rice is tender to bite (about 10 more minutes). Let cool; cover and refrigerate for up to 1 day. (Or freeze for up to 4 months. Thaw overnight in refrigerator; or defrost in a microwave following manufacturer's directions.)

To serve: Bring to room temperature and serve; or reheat, covered, over medium heat for about 10 minutes, stirring once or twice.

Add chopped mint leaves and lemon juice to rice mixture and stir gently to blend; season to taste with salt and pepper. Garnish with mint sprigs. Makes 6 to 8 servings.

Tomato-smothered Leeks

Initial preparation: About 45 minutes
Storage time: 1 day
Final preparation: None

Per serving: 107 calories, 2 g protein, 17 g carbohydrates, 4 g total fat, 0 mg cholesterol, 386 mg sodium

Slender leeks are bathed in a tomato sauce influenced by the sunny flavors of southern Italy.

- 9 medium-size leeks (about 2¾ lbs. *total*)
- 2 tablespoons olive oil
- 2 cloves garlic, minced or pressed
- 2 cans (about 15 oz. *each*) stewed tomatoes
- ¼ cup sliced ripe olives
- ¾ teaspoon *each* dry basil, dry rosemary, dry marjoram, and dry oregano leaves
- ¼ teaspoon freshly ground pepper

Make-ahead steps: Cut off and discard root ends of leeks. Trim tops, leaving about 1½ inches of green leaves. Strip away and discard coarse outer leaves. Split leeks in half lengthwise. Rinse well, keeping halves intact.

Pour water to a depth of ½ inch into a 12- to 14-inch frying pan and bring to a boil over medium-high heat. Lay leeks side by side in pan without crowding; cook, covered, until just tender when pierced (3 to 5 minutes). Lift leeks from pan and set aside until cool. Repeat for remaining leeks. Cover and refrigerate for up to 1 day.

Heat oil in a 12- to 14-inch frying pan over medium heat. When oil is hot, add garlic and cook, stirring, for 1 minute. Stir in tomatoes (break up with a spoon) and their liquid, olives, basil, rosemary, marjoram, oregano, and pepper. Bring to a boil. Reduce heat and simmer, uncovered, until sauce is reduced to 2 cups (about 15 minutes). Cover and refrigerate for up to 1 day.

To serve: Arrange leeks on a platter and pour on tomato sauce. Makes 6 to 8 servings.

Bathed in a light sauce, plump bulbs of Fennel Orange Gratin (recipe on facing page) are gilded at the last minute with Swiss cheese and grated orange peel. Feathery fennel leaves lend a garnish.

Pictured on facing page

Fennel Orange Gratin

Initial preparation: *About 45 minutes*
Storage time: *1 day*
Final preparation: *About 5 minutes*

Per serving: 171 calories, 5 g protein, 7 g carbohydrates, 15 g total fat, 38 mg cholesterol, 677 mg sodium

In this elegant side dish, the licorice flavor of slowly simmered fennel is complemented by an orange- and cinnamon-scented sauce. Topped with cheese, the dish is broiled until golden just before serving.

> 2 **small heads fennel or 1 large head fennel (about 1 lb. *total*)**
> 1¾ **cups regular-strength chicken broth**
> ¼ **cup butter or margarine**
> 1½ **tablespoons all-purpose flour**
> ¼ **teaspoon ground cinnamon**
> 1 **teaspoon grated orange peel**
> ¼ **cup Swiss cheese, shredded Freshly ground pepper**

Make-ahead steps: Cut fennel in half lengthwise. Cut off and discard woody stems and bruises. Cut off feathery fennel leaves and set aside.

In a 3- to 4-quart pan, bring broth to a boil over medium-high heat. Add fennel; reduce heat, cover, and simmer until tender when pierced (about 20 minutes for small heads; 30 minutes for large head). Drain, reserving broth.

In a 2- to 3-quart pan, melt butter over medium-high heat; add flour. Cook, stirring, until flour and butter are lightly browned (about 3 minutes). Remove from heat and stir in 1 cup reserved broth; return to heat and cook until thickened (about 3 minutes). Stir in cinnamon and ½ teaspoon of the orange peel.

Pour sauce into a 9- by 13-inch baking dish and place fennel on top, cut side down. If using one large fennel, cut each half lengthwise. Top fennel, except for stalk tips, with cheese. Cover and refrigerate for up to 1 day.

To serve: Broil about 4 inches from heat until browned (about 5 minutes). Garnish fennel with reserved leaves and sprinkle with remaining ½ teaspoon orange peel. Season to taste with pepper. Makes 4 servings.

Pictured on front cover

Glazed Roasted Onions

Initial preparation: *About 10 minutes*
Storage time: *1 day*
Final preparation: *About 1 hour*

Per serving: 34 calories, .94 g protein, 7 g carbohydrates, .20 g total fat, 0 mg cholesterol, 70 mg sodium

Slowly baked in a glorious sweet and sour sauce, our glazed onion halves may steal center stage from your entrée of grilled beef or turkey.

> 1½ **cups water**
> 1 **cup balsamic vinegar or red wine vinegar**
> 4 **teaspoons firmly packed brown sugar**
> **About ½ teaspoon salt**
> ¼ **teaspoon pepper**
> 8 **medium-size onions**

Make-ahead steps: Blend water, vinegar, and sugar; add ½ teaspoon of the salt and pepper. Pour equal amounts into two 9- by 13-inch baking pans. Cut onions in half lengthwise, through skins. Place, cut sides down, in vinegar mixture. Cover and refrigerate for up to 1 day.

To serve: Uncover and bake in lower third of a 400° oven until onions give readily when gently squeezed, most of the liquid has evaporated, and cut sides of onions are glazed (about 1 hour). Arrange, cut side up, on a platter. Season to taste with salt. Makes 8 or 16 servings.

Do-Ahead Dressings

With an exquisite dressing, any salad can be a work of art. You can enjoy a salad masterpiece on any evening by creating these dressings ahead and keeping them on hand. *Most can be conveniently stored for up to two weeks.*

Fresh Orange & Yogurt, Poppy Seed, and Wine Grape dressings bring out the best of fruit salads; Berry Vinegar Vinaigrette, Garlic Cream, Chinese Mustard, Thick Green Onion, and Green Goddess dressings turn salad greens and vegetables into *chefs d'oeuvres.*

Our Passion Fruit Dressing goes equally well with fruit and vegetables.

Passion Fruit Dressing

- ¼ cup passion fruit pulp, including seeds (2 to 3 fruits)
- 6 tablespoons lemon juice
- 2 tablespoons sugar
- 1 teaspoon *each* grated lemon peel and dry mustard
- ¾ cup salad oil

In a food processor or blender, whirl pulp until seeds resemble coarsely ground pepper. Add lemon juice, sugar, lemon peel, and dry mustard; whirl until blended. With motor running, gradually add oil in a thin, steady stream until incorporated. Cover and refrigerate for up to 3 days. Makes about 1¼ cups.

Per tablespoon: 80 calories, .06 g protein, 2 g carbohydrates, 8 g total fat, 0 mg cholesterol, 1 mg sodium

Fresh Orange & Yogurt Dressing

- 1 large orange
- 1 tablespoon cornstarch
- 2 tablespoons sugar
- ½ cup plain yogurt

With a vegetable peeler, pare off orange-colored layer of orange peel; cut into very thin shreds. Ream orange to make ⅔ cup juice. Mix juice with cornstarch and set aside.

In a 1- to 1½-quart pan, boil orange peel in 1 cup water over high heat for 1 minute; drain. Repeat.

Add sugar and ½ cup water to drained peel. Boil, uncovered, over high heat, stirring, until peel is translucent and syrup is reduced to about 1 tablespoon. Add orange juice mixture and bring to a boil. Let cool. Stir yogurt into orange sauce. Cover tightly and refrigerate for up to 2 weeks. Makes about 1 cup.

Per tablespoon: 18 calories, .45 g protein, 4 g carbohydrates, .12 g total fat, .42 mg cholesterol, 5 mg sodium

Berry Vinegar Vinaigrette

- 5 tablespoons raspberry or blueberry vinegar
- ½ cup olive oil or salad oil
- 2 tablespoons minced shallots
- 1 teaspoon Dijon mustard
- 1 teaspoon honey
- Freshly ground pepper

Pour vinegar, oil, shallots, mustard, and honey into a small jar; shake to mix. Season to taste with pepper. Cover tightly and refrigerate for up to 2 weeks. Makes 1 cup.

Per tablespoon: 63 calories, .03 g protein, .88 g carbohydrates, 7 g total fat, 0 mg cholesterol, 10 mg sodium

Green Goddess Dressing

- 3 large egg yolks
- 3 tablespoons white wine vinegar
- ⅔ cup lightly packed chopped parsley
- 1 can (2 oz.) anchovy fillets, including oil
- 6 green onions (including tops), chopped
- 1½ teaspoons dry tarragon, crumbled
- 1¼ cups salad oil

In a blender, combine egg yolks, vinegar, parsley, anchovy fillets, green onions, and tarragon; whirl until puréed. With motor running, gradually add oil in a thin, steady stream until well blended. Cover and refrigerate for up to 1 week. Makes 1½ cups.

Per tablespoon: 119 calories, 1 g protein, .46 g carbohydrates, 13 g total fat, 35 mg cholesterol, 71 mg sodium

Chinese Mustard Dressing

4 teaspoons prepared Chinese mustard or Dijon mustard
¼ cup lemon juice
1 teaspoon Worcestershire
½ cup olive oil or salad oil
3 tablespoons grated Parmesan cheese
　Freshly ground pepper

In a small bowl, whisk together mustard, lemon juice, Worcestershire, oil, and cheese until slightly thick and creamy. Season to taste with pepper. Cover tightly and refrigerate for up to 2 weeks. Makes about 1 cup.

Per tablespoon: 67 calories, .40 g protein, .49 g carbohydrates, 7 g total fat, .74 mg cholesterol, 59 mg sodium

Wine Grape Dressing

2 tablespoons plain yogurt
2 tablespoons minced crystallized ginger
¼ teaspoon paprika
½ cup white wine grape juice, such as White Riesling or Gewürztraminer, or white grape juice
3 tablespoons white wine vinegar
1 tablespoon salad oil

In a bowl, whisk yogurt, ginger, and paprika until blended. Continue to whisk and pour in juice, vinegar, and oil. Cover and refrigerate for up to 2 weeks. Makes ¾ cup.

Per tablespoon: 27 calories, .13 g protein, 4 g carbohydrates, 1 g total fat, .14 mg cholesterol, 3 mg sodium

Poppy Seed Dressing

⅓ cup *each* red wine vinegar and salad oil
¼ cup honey
4 teaspoons *each* poppy seeds and minced onion
¾ teaspoon ground mace
　Salt

In a small bowl, stir together vinegar, oil, honey, poppy seeds, minced onion, and mace until slightly thick and creamy. Season to taste with salt. Cover and refrigerate for up to 2 weeks. Makes about 1 cup.

Per tablespoon: 61 calories, .14 g protein, 5 g carbohydrates, 5 g total fat, 0 mg cholesterol, .48 mg sodium

Thick Green Onion Dressing

½ cup coarsely chopped green onions (including tops)
¼ cup mayonnaise
1 clove garlic
1 tablespoon *each* white wine vinegar and Dijon mustard
¼ teaspoon pepper
¾ cup sour cream

In a food processor or blender, combine green onions, mayonnaise, garlic, vinegar, mustard, and pepper; whirl until green onions are puréed. Stir in sour cream. Cover and refrigerate for up to 3 days. Makes about 1 cup.

Per tablespoon: 50 calories, .43 g protein, .95 g carbohydrates, 5 g total fat, 7 mg cholesterol, 54 mg sodium

Garlic Cream Dressing

½ cup red wine vinegar
3 tablespoons Dijon mustard
1 large egg
3 cloves garlic
⅛ teaspoon liquid hot pepper seasoning
1½ teaspoons sugar
1½ cups olive oil
　Freshly ground pepper

In a blender or food processor, combine vinegar, mustard, egg, garlic, liquid hot pepper seasoning, and sugar; whirl until garlic is puréed. With motor running, gradually add oil in a thin, steady stream until incorporated; season to taste with pepper. Cover tightly and refrigerate for up to 2 weeks. Makes about 2½ cups.

Per tablespoon: 76 calories, .16 g protein, .47 g carbohydrates, 8 g total fat, 7 mg cholesterol, 36 mg sodium

Pictured on facing page

Sweet Potatoes Anna

Initial preparation: *About 30 minutes*

Storage time: *1 day in refrigerator; 10 months in freezer*

Final preparation: *About 1½ hours*

Per serving: 273 calories, 4 g protein, 27 g carbohydrates, 17 g total fat, 45 mg cholesterol, 263 mg sodium

Paper-thin slices of sweet potato, laced with butter and cheese, bake into an elegant cake. Unlike most white potatoes used in this classic recipe, the orange-fleshed sweet potato doesn't discolor quickly, a convenience for the make-ahead cook.

> **2 pounds sweet potatoes (about 4 medium-size)**
> **½ cup (¼ lb.) butter or margarine, melted**
> **6 tablespoons grated Parmesan cheese**
> **Salt and pepper**

Make-ahead steps: Peel potatoes. Using a food processor or thin-bladed sharp knife, slice potatoes into paper-thin (about ⅛-inch) slices. Completely coat bottom of a 9-inch round baking pan with 1 tablespoon of the butter.

Arrange ⅙ of the slices in an overlapping layer on bottom of pan. Drizzle with another tablespoon of the butter and sprinkle with about 1 tablespoon of the cheese; then sprinkle lightly with salt and pepper. Repeat layers until all ingredients are used; drizzle top with any remaining butter. Cover with foil. Push down on potatoes with your hands to compress. Refrigerate for up to 1 day. (Or freeze for up to 10 months. Thaw overnight in refrigerator; or defrost in a microwave following manufacturer's directions.)

To serve: Bake on lowest rack of a 425° oven for 45 minutes. Uncover and continue baking until potatoes are brown and crisp on top and edges (about 40 minutes). Let stand for 5 minutes.

Using a large spatula to hold potatoes in place, drain off excess butter. Loosen potatoes around edges; invert onto a platter. Cut into wedges. Makes 6 servings.

Pictured on page 26

Summer Squash Gratin

Initial preparation: *About 1¼ hours*

Storage time: *1 day*

Final preparation: *About 1 hour and 20 minutes*

Per serving: 167 calories, 5 g protein, 16 g carbohydrates, 11 g total fat, 4 mg cholesterol, 103 mg sodium

Bell pepper rings, combined with slices of summer squash, create a colorful topping for this baked vegetable dish. The sweet, slowly cooked blend of onions, eggplant, and tomatoes may remind you of ratatouille. Vary the casserole's appearance by the colors of squash and pepper you choose.

> **5 tablespoons olive oil or salad oil**
> **2 large onions, sliced**
> **2 eggplants (about 1½ lbs. *total*), cut into ½-inch cubes**
> **½ teaspoon ground sage**
> **¾ teaspoon dry thyme leaves**
> **2 large tomatoes, chopped**
> **Salt and pepper**

> **1½ pounds summer squash (crookneck, pattypan, or zucchini), ends trimmed, cut crosswise into ¼-inch slices**
> **¾ to 1 pound small red, green, or yellow bell peppers, seeded and cut into ¼-inch slices**
> **½ cup Parmesan cheese**

Make-ahead steps: Heat 4 tablespoons of the oil in a 10- to 12-inch frying pan over medium heat. When oil is hot, add onions, eggplants, sage, and ½ teaspoon of the thyme. Cook uncovered, stirring often, until liquid has evaporated, onions are pale gold, and eggplants begin to fall apart (about 40 minutes).

Add tomatoes and cook over high heat, stirring, until liquid has evaporated. Season to taste with salt and pepper. Spoon vegetables evenly into a shallow 2½- to 3-quart rectangular or oval baking pan.

Sprinkle squash slices lightly with salt, pepper, and remaining ¼ teaspoon thyme. Arrange squash and bell peppers on onion mixture, alternating rows; sprinkle with remaining oil. Cover and refrigerate for up to 1 day.

To serve: Uncover and bake in a 350° oven until squash is tender-crisp when pierced (about 1¼ hours). Sprinkle with cheese and bake until lightly browned (about 5 minutes). Serve hot or at room temperature. Makes 8 servings.

Dress up your next roast beef dinner with golden Sweet Potatoes Anna
(recipe on facing page) and vivid green Asparagus with Oranges (recipe on
page 64). Both complement the roast with fresh color and flavor, as they
offer you make-ahead convenience.

Breads

 What could taste better than homemade bread? Made-ahead-at-home bread, that's what! This chapter presents a variety of such breads to make and eat at your convenience. Bake hearty Vegetable-patch Bread when planning a picnic; serve delicate Gravenstein Apple Bread with your favorite tea; choose Ready-to-Go Rolls for a mid-week treat; offer slices of Fresh Rosemary Flatbread with cold cuts and relish; and offer French Walnut Bread with a favorite cheese.

Fresh Rosemary Flatbread

Initial preparation: *About 1 hour, plus about 1 hour for rising*

Storage time: *1 day at room temperature; 4 months in freezer*

Final preparation: *None*

Per serving: 90 calories, 3 g protein, 16 g carbohydrates, 1 g total fat, 18 mg cholesterol, 296 mg sodium

This circular loaf brings elegance to any sandwich. Fresh rosemary pressed into the dough adds bursts of flavor.

- **8 to 10 fresh rosemary sprigs (*each* 6 to 8 inches long) or 2 teaspoons dry rosemary**
- **1 package active dry yeast**
- **1 cup warm water (about 110° F)**
- **1 tablespoon olive oil or salad oil**
- **2¼ cups all-purpose flour**
- **1 egg yolk beaten with 1 tablespoon water**
- **1 tablespoon coarse salt**

Make-ahead steps: Set aside 2 of the rosemary sprigs. Strip leaves off remaining sprigs and coarsely chop enough to make 2 tablespoons.

In a bowl, sprinkle yeast over warm water; let stand until softened. Stir in chopped rosemary, oil, and 1½ cups of the flour.

Mix in enough of the remaining ¾ cup flour to form a soft dough. Knead on a floured board (or knead with a dough hook) until dough is smooth (about 10 minutes; 5 minutes on high speed with a dough hook), adding flour as needed.

Place dough in a greased bowl; turn to grease top. Cover and let rise in a warm place until doubled (about 45 minutes).

Punch dough down and knead briefly on a floured board to release air. Roll out dough into a 12-inch round on an oiled 12- by 15-inch baking sheet or 14-inch pizza pan. With your fingers, poke indentations about 1 inch apart all over top.

Let rise, uncovered, in a warm place until puffy (about 15 minutes). Brush with egg yolk glaze and sprinkle with salt. Lay reserved rosemary sprigs in center; press lightly into dough.

Bake in a 375° oven until golden (about 40 minutes). Let cool on a rack; wrap airtight and store at room temperature for up to 1 day. (Or freeze for up to 4 months. Thaw at room temperature for 4 to 5 hours.) Makes 1 loaf (about 15 servings).

French Walnut Bread

Initial preparation: *About 45 minutes, plus about 30 minutes for rising*

Storage time: *3 days at room temperature; 6 months in freezer*

Final preparation: *None*

Per serving: 86 calories, 2 g protein, 11 g carbohydrates, 4 g total fat, 1 mg cholesterol, 74 mg sodium

This dense walnut loaf is a version of a bread often served with the cheese course in France. The rye-based dough is kneaded briefly, just until it feels smooth. This recipe makes 2 loaves.

- **1 cup coarsely broken walnuts**
- **1 package active dry yeast**
- **1 cup warm water (about 110°F)**
- **¾ teaspoon salt**
- **1 teaspoon sugar**
- **1½ cups rye flour**
- **About 1½ cups all-purpose flour**
- **1 tablespoon butter or margarine, melted**

Make-ahead steps: Place walnuts in a 9-inch baking pan. Bake in a 350° oven until lightly toasted, shaking often (10 to 12 minutes). Let cool.

In a large bowl, sprinkle yeast over warm water; let stand until softened. Stir in salt, sugar, rye flour, 1⅓ cups of the all-purpose flour, and walnuts. Mix well.

Knead on a floured board, adding flour as needed, until dough is smooth and no longer sticky when lightly touched (about 10 minutes). Divide dough in half. Shape each portion into a 2- by 10-inch log; place about 4 inches apart on a greased 12- by 15-inch baking sheet. Cover lightly with plastic wrap and let rise in a warm place until slightly puffy (about 30 minutes).

Uncover loaves and brush tops with melted butter. Bake in a 425° oven until well browned (about 20 minutes). Transfer from pan to a rack. Let cool; wrap airtight and store at room temperature for up to 3 days. (Or freeze for up to 6 months. Thaw at room temperature for 4 to 5 hours.) Makes 2 loaves (each about 12 servings).

One wonderful way to eat vegetables is offered by our crusty
Vegetable-patch Bread (recipe on facing page). It bursts with garden-fresh
bounty, including carrots, tomatoes, broccoli, and bell peppers.

Vegetable-patch Bread

Initial preparation: *About 1½ hours, plus about 2 hours for rising*
Storage time: *3 days in refrigerator; 6 months in freezer*
Final preparation: *None*

Per serving: 181 calories, 6 g protein, 30 g carbohydrates, 4 g total fat, 21 mg cholesterol, 117 mg sodium

Bursting with vegetables, this colorful loaf shows off gifts from your garden or market.

    Garden Vegetables (recipe follows)
1 **package active dry yeast**
¾ **cup warm water (about 110°F)**
1 **large egg**
½ **teaspoon salt**
1 **tablespoon sugar**
1 **tablespoon *each* minced fresh thyme and tarragon leaves or 1 teaspoon *each* dry thyme and dry tarragon leaves**
¼ **cup minced fresh basil leaves or 1½ tablespoons dry basil**
1 **tablespoon olive oil**
¼ **cup grated Parmesan cheese**
1 **cup whole wheat flour**
    About 3 cups all-purpose flour

Make-ahead steps: Prepare Garden Vegetables; set aside.

In a large bowl, sprinkle yeast over water; let stand until softened. Mix in egg, salt, sugar, thyme, tarragon, basil, oil, cheese, whole-wheat flour, and 1⅔ cups of the all-purpose flour until blended.

Knead on a floured board until smooth (8 to 12 minutes), adding flour as needed. Mix vegetables with ½ cup of the remaining all-purpose flour. Knead vegetables into dough, adding flour as needed. Place in an oiled bowl; turn to grease top. Cover and let rise in a warm place until doubled (about 1½ hours).

Punch down and knead briefly on a floured board, adding flour until dough is soft but not sticky. Shape into a 6- to 7-inch round; place on a greased 12- by 15-inch baking sheet. Cover and let rise until puffy (about 30 minutes). Uncover and bake in a 350° oven until browned (40 to 45 minutes). Let cool on a rack. Wrap airtight and refrigerate for up to 3 days. (Or freeze for up to 6 months. Thaw overnight in refrigerator.) Makes 1 loaf (about 14 servings).

Garden Vegetables. In a wide frying pan, cook 1 **onion,** halved and cut ¾ inch thick; 2 cloves **garlic,** minced or pressed; ½ cup chopped **eggplant;** and 2 tablespoons **olive oil** or salad oil over medium heat, stirring often, until eggplant is barely tender (about 10 minutes). Add ⅓ cup chopped **pear-shaped tomatoes;** cook, stirring, until tomatoes are slightly soft (1 to 2 minutes). Let cool.

Cut 1 quarter *each* of a **red and green bell pepper** into thin strips. Diagonally cut ¾ inch thick 1 **carrot,** 1 stalk **celery,** and 1 **zucchini;** cut 2 **green onions** 4 inches thick. Bring 3 cups **water** to a boil over high heat. Cook carrots and ¾ cup **broccoli flowerets** for 1 minute, zucchini and bell peppers for 45 seconds, and celery and green onions for 30 seconds. Drain, place in ice water; drain again. Pat dry. Add to tomato mixture.

Ready-to-Go Rolls

Initial preparation: *About 20 minutes*
Storage time: *1 day*
Final preparation: *About 30 minutes, plus about 20 minutes for rising*

Per roll: 172 calories, 4 g protein, 26 g carbohydrates, 5 g total fat, 24 mg cholesterol, 55 mg sodium

Make this dough ahead; shape and bake the next day.

2 **packages active dry yeast**
½ **cup warm water (about 110° F)**
½ **cup *each* milk, salad oil, and sugar**
½ **teaspoon salt**
2 **eggs**
    About 5½ cups all-purpose flour

Make-ahead steps: In large bowl of an electric mixer, sprinkle yeast over water; let stand until softened. Add milk, oil, sugar, salt, eggs, and 3 cups of the flour. Beat on medium speed for 5 minutes. Stir in 2 more cups of the flour.

Knead on a floured board until smooth (about 5 minutes), adding flour as needed. Place in a greased bowl; turn to grease top. Cover and refrigerate for up to 1 day.

To serve: Punch down and knead briefly. Cut into 24 pieces, shaping each into a smooth ball. Arrange 2 inches apart on 2 greased 11- by 17-inch baking sheets. Cover and let rise in a warm place until puffy (about 20 minutes). Uncover and bake in a 350° oven until golden (about 15 minutes). Makes 2 dozen.

Beat-the-Clock Breakfasts

Sunrise; another day begins. Wouldn't it be wonderful to wake to a leisurely breakfast without the usual morning rush? How about a breakfast of fresh-baked waffles served with sweet honey syrup, sugared bacon, and plump poached prunes topped with vanilla custard? Maybe you'd choose hearty buckwheat crêpes with pears instead. Crunchy chunks of oatmeal and peanut butter or fruit-studded bran muffins provide a healthy morning start. Here's how it's done: you make all or most of the meal the night before; then enjoy a sumptuous breakfast in bed.

Overnight Waffles with Dutch Honey

Dutch Honey (recipe follows)
1 package active dry yeast
1 teaspoon sugar
2½ cups warm water (about 110°F)
⅔ cup low-fat dry milk
About ⅓ cup salad oil
½ teaspoon *each* baking soda and salt
2 large eggs
3 cups all-purpose flour

Make-ahead steps: Prepare Dutch Honey.

Dissolve yeast and sugar in warm water; let stand until bubbly (about 5 minutes). Add dry milk, ⅓ cup of the oil, baking soda, salt, eggs, and flour; beat until smooth. Cover and refrigerate for up to 5 days. (Or freeze for up to 1 month. Thaw overnight in refrigerator; or

defrost in a microwave following manufacturer's directions.)

To serve: Heat an electric waffle iron to medium-hot or place a waffle iron over medium heat. If needed, brush grid with oil. Stir batter and pour into center of grid (¾ cup for a standard 9-inch iron). Cook until browned (about 3 minutes); repeat for desired number of waffles. Serve hot with honey. Makes 7 or 8 waffles.

Dutch Honey. In a 2- to 3-quart pan, combine 1 cup **sugar,** 1 cup **whipping cream,** and 1 cup **maple syrup;** bring to a boil over medium heat. Let cool; cover and refrigerate for up to 1 week. Reheat over medium heat. Makes 8 servings.

Per serving: 577 calories, 9 g protein, 91 g carbohydrates, 20 g total fat, 103 mg cholesterol, 252 mg sodium

Bran Apple Muffins

1 cup *each* bran cereal and untoasted wheat germ
1½ cups whole-wheat flour
½ cup nonfat dry milk
1 tablespoon baking powder
¾ cup raisins
½ cup chopped walnuts
2 large eggs
12 ounces thawed frozen apple juice concentrate
¼ cup salad oil

Make-ahead steps: In a large bowl, mix bran cereal, wheat germ, flour, dry milk, baking powder, raisins, and walnuts.

In a small bowl, beat eggs, apple juice concentrate, and oil. Add to dry ingredients and mix well. Let stand until moisture is absorbed (about 5 minutes).

Spoon batter into paper-lined or greased muffin cups (2½ inches wide), filling to rim. Bake in a 375° oven until tinged a dark golden brown (about 30 minutes). Transfer from pan to a rack. Let cool; wrap airtight and store at room temperature for up to 1 day. (Or freeze for up to 6 months. Thaw at room temperature for 4 to 5 hours.) Makes 12 muffins.

Per muffin: 285 calories, 9 g protein, 45 g carbohydrates, 10 g total fat, 46 mg cholesterol, 225 mg sodium

Buckwheat Crêpes with Pears

1⅓ cups milk
4 large eggs
1 cup buckwheat flour
About 2 tablespoons butter or margarine
12 to 15 pecan or walnut halves
4 or 5 small, soft-ripe Comice or Anjou pears, cored and sliced
Sour cream
Warm maple syrup

Make-ahead steps: In a blender, combine milk, eggs, and flour; whirl until smooth. Place a 7- to 8-inch crêpe pan or frying pan over medium-high heat. When hot, add ¼ teaspoon of the butter and swirl to coat surface. Stir batter and pour about ¼ cup into frying pan, quickly tilting pan so batter flows evenly over bottom. Cook until top is dry and edge is lightly browned (about 1 minute). Turn with a spatula and brown other side (about 30 more seconds).

Turn out onto a plate and fold in quarters to make a triangle. Repeat to make remaining crêpes. Place folded crêpes in a single layer on two 12- by 15-inch baking sheets.

In same pan, melt remaining butter over medium-low heat. Quickly add nuts and cook, shaking often, until lightly toasted (2 to 3 minutes). Scatter nuts over crêpes. Let cool; cover and refrigerate for up to 1 day.

To serve: Bake, covered, in a 400° oven until hot (5 to 8 minutes). Top each serving with pears, sour cream, and syrup. Makes about 4 servings (16 crêpes).

Per crêpe: 357 calories, 12 g protein, 41 g carbohydrates, 17 g total fat, 301 mg cholesterol, 168 mg sodium

Oatmeal-Peanut Breakfast Chunks

- 1 cup (½ lb.) butter or margarine, at room temperature
- ¾ cup *each* firmly packed brown sugar and crunchy peanut butter
- ½ cup honey
- 2 large eggs
- 2 teaspoons vanilla
- 1½ cups whole-wheat flour
- 3½ cups rolled oats
- 1 teaspoon baking soda
- 1 cup chopped dried apricots or chopped pitted prunes

Make-ahead steps: In a food processor, combine butter, brown sugar, peanut butter, honey, eggs, and vanilla; whirl until smooth.

In a large bowl, mix flour, oats, and baking soda. Add dry ingredients to butter mixture and whirl to mix (or beat with an electric mixer). Stir in apricots.

Spread batter evenly in a 9- by 13-inch baking pan. Bake in a

325° oven until edges are lightly browned and center feels slightly soft when pressed (25 to 30 minutes). Let cool in pan on a rack. Cut into 2-inch squares. Wrap airtight and store at room temperature for up to 1 week. (Or freeze for up to 6 months. Thaw at room temperature for 4 to 5 hours.) Makes 10 to 15 servings.

Per serving: 406 calories, 9 g protein, 48 g carbohydrates, 21 g total fat, 70 mg cholesterol, 247 mg sodium

Prunes with Two Sauces

- 3 tablespoons oolong or orange pekoe tea leaves
- 2 cups (about ½ lb.) prunes with pits
- 2 cups dry white wine or water
- 1 cup water
- ½ cup sugar
- 1 slice lemon peel, yellow part only (about ½ inch wide and 4 inches long)
  Vanilla Custard (recipe follows)

Make-ahead steps: Place tea leaves in a tea ball or tie up in a small rectangle of cheesecloth. In a 2- to 3-quart pan, combine tea leaves, prunes, wine, water, sugar, and lemon peel. Cover and bring to a boil over medium-high heat. Reduce heat to just under a simmer and cook until prunes are slightly plumped (about 1 hour).

With a slotted spoon, remove prunes; set aside. Lift out and discard tea leaves. Boil syrup over medium-high heat until reduced to ¾ cup. Return prunes to syrup. Cover and refrigerate for up to 4 days. (Or freeze for up to 6 months. Thaw overnight in refrigerator; or defrost in a microwave following manufacturer's directions.)

Prepare Vanilla Custard.

To serve: Return prunes and custard to room temperature. Serve prunes with syrup and custard. Makes 4 servings.

Vanilla Custard. In a 1- to 2-quart pan, combine 2 tablespoons **sugar** with 3 **egg yolks;** stir until blended. Add ¾ cup **milk** and a 6-inch piece split **vanilla bean** (or add vanilla later) and cook over medium heat. Continue to cook, stirring constantly, until custard coats back of a metal spoon in a smooth, thin layer (about 5 minutes). Do not allow custard to scald or it will curdle.

Remove from heat and lift out vanilla bean (or add ½ teaspoon vanilla); strain custard, if desired. Let cool; cover and refrigerate for up to 2 days.

Per serving: 323 calories, 5 g protein, 66 g carbohydrates, 6 g total fat, 211 mg cholesterol, 42 mg sodium

Sugared Bacon

- 8 to 12 slices bacon
- 3 tablespoons firmly packed brown sugar

Make-ahead steps: Line a 10- by 15-inch baking pan with foil. Lay bacon slices on foil. Bake, uncovered, in a 350° oven for 10 minutes. Remove pan from oven; drain off and discard fat.

Evenly sprinkle bacon with sugar; then smooth with back of a spoon. Let cool. Cover and refrigerate for up to 1 day. (Or freeze for up to 1 month. Thaw overnight in refrigerator; or defrost in a microwave following manufacturer's directions.)

To serve: Uncover and bake in a 350° oven until golden brown (about 15 more minutes). Transfer with tongs or a wide spatula and arrange, sugared sides up, in a single layer on a rack over paper towels. Serve cool. Makes 4 servings.

Per serving: 111 calories, 4 g protein, 10 g carbohydrates, 6 g total fat, 11 mg cholesterol, 205 mg sodium

Gravenstein Apple Bread

Initial preparation: About 1½ hours
Storage time: 5 days in refrigerator; 10 months in freezer
Final preparation: None

Per serving: 358 calories, 5 g protein, 51 g carbohydrates, 16 g total fat, 86 mg cholesterol, 169 mg sodium

Enjoy the tart sweetness of Gravenstein apples in this cinnamon-spiced bread, loaded with raisins.

> 3 **cups all-purpose flour**
> 2½ **teaspoons ground cinnamon**
> 1¼ **teaspoons baking soda**
> ½ **teaspoon baking powder**
> ½ **teaspoon salt**
> 2 **cups granulated sugar**
> 1 **can (1 lb.) Gravenstein applesauce**
> 1 **cup salad oil**
> 5 **large eggs**
> 1 **tablespoon vanilla**
> ½ **cup raisins**
> 2 **teaspoons firmly packed brown sugar**

Make-ahead steps: In a bowl, mix flour, cinnamon, baking soda, baking powder, and salt. Set aside.

In large bowl of an electric mixer, combine granulated sugar, applesauce, oil, eggs, and vanilla. Beat on low speed until well blended; then beat on high speed for 2 minutes.

Add dry ingredients to batter and beat on low speed until well combined; stir in raisins. Spoon batter equally into 2 well-greased 5- by 9-inch loaf pans. Evenly sprinkle each loaf with 1 teaspoon of the brown sugar.

Bake in a 325° oven until a wooden pick inserted in center comes out clean (about 1¼ hours). Let cool in pans for 15 minutes; then invert from pans onto racks. Let cool, wrap airtight, and refrigerate for up to 5 days. (Or freeze for up to 10 months. Thaw overnight in refrigerator; or defrost in a microwave following manufacturer's directions.) Makes 2 loaves (each about 16 servings).

Pictured on facing page

Fresh Corn Madeleines

Initial preparation: 20 to 35 minutes
Storage time: 1 day at room temperature; 1 month in freezer
Final preparation: About 10 minutes

Per madeleine: 52 calories, 1 g protein, 7 g carbohydrates, 2 g total fat, 13 mg cholesterol, 89 mg sodium

Shell-shaped madeleine pans, usually reserved for French dessert cookies, turn out corn muffins in elegant form. These "muff-eleines" include corn kernels as a tender foil for the coarse and crunchy polenta (Italian-style cornmeal).

> About ⅓ **cup butter or margarine**
> 1 **small onion, minced**
> 1 **cup all-purpose flour**
> About 1 **cup polenta or yellow cornmeal**
> 1 **tablespoon baking powder**
> ½ **teaspoon salt**
> 1 **large egg**
> 1 **cup milk**
> 1 **cup fresh or frozen and thawed corn kernels**

Make-ahead steps: In a 10- to 12-inch frying pan, melt ⅓ cup of the butter over medium-high heat. Add onion and cook, stirring occasionally, until soft (about 5 minutes); set aside.

In a bowl, blend flour, 1 cup of the polenta, baking powder, and salt. In another bowl, whisk egg and milk until blended. Stir minced onion, milk mixture, and corn into flour mixture just until blended.

Butter madeleine pans (each 1½- to 2-tablespoon size) or petite muffin pans (about 1½ inches wide). Sprinkle pans with polenta; shake out excess. Spoon batter into pans, filling to rim.

Bake in a 350° oven until firm to touch (about 10 minutes for 1½-tablespoon size, 15 minutes for 2-tablespoon size, or 25 minutes for muffins). Let cool slightly; then invert from pans onto racks, easing madeleines free with a thin spatula, if necessary. Let cool; wrap airtight and store at room temperature for up to 1 day. (Or freeze for up to 1 month. Thaw at room temperature for 4 to 5 hours.)

To serve: Bring to room temperature and serve; or, to reheat, lay madeleines in a 10- by 15-inch pan and place in a 300° oven until warm in center (about 10 minutes). Makes 2 to 3 dozen madeleines.

Golden, kernel-filled cornbread adopts an elegant French shape in
Fresh Corn Madeleines (recipe on facing page). Serve, warm from the oven,
with butter, jam, or jalapeño jelly.

Desserts

Do you find sweets too tempting to resist after you make them? This chapter offers many such temptations, all prepared in advance. But it gives no advice on how to avoid nibbling before serving. Among the desserts that may test your willpower are chocolate-filled Brandied Toffee Lace, buttery Ginger Shortbread Wedges, festive Pumpkin Cheesecake Tart, fruit-laden White Chocolate Fruit Terrine, and light Melon-Mint Sorbet. Try them all, and more. Just be sure to leave a few portions for your guests.

Sublime Brown Sugar Bars

Initial preparation: *About 50 minutes*
Storage time: *3 days at room temperature; 6 months in freezer*
Final preparation: *None*

Per bar: 140 calories, 2 g protein, 18 g carbohydrates, 7 g total fat, 25 mg cholesterol, 75 mg sodium

Simple brown sugar cookies become complex with sensational taste and texture when packed with oats, nuts, raisins, and coconut. Stock the cookie jar now; serve with vanilla ice cream later.

- 1 **cup (½ lb.) butter or margarine**
- 1 **cup** *each* **granulated and firmly packed brown sugar**
- 2 **large eggs**
- 2 **teaspoons vanilla**
- 1 **tablespoon light molasses**
- 2 **cups all-purpose flour**
- 1 **cup regular or quick-cooking rolled oats**
- 1 **teaspoon baking soda**
- ½ **teaspoon baking powder**
- ½ **cup raisins**
- ½ **cup chopped pecans, walnuts, or almonds**
- 1½ **cups sweetened shredded coconut**

Make-ahead steps: In a large bowl, beat butter, granulated sugar, and brown sugar until creamy. Mix in eggs, vanilla, and molasses.

In another bowl, combine flour, oats, baking soda, and baking powder. Add to butter mixture, blending well. Stir in raisins, nuts, and coconut.

Spread mixture in a buttered 10- by 15-inch baking pan. Bake in a 350° oven until center feels set when lightly touched (about 40 minutes). Let cool on a rack, cut into bars, and place in an airtight container. Store at room temperature for up to 3 days. (Or freeze for up to 6 months. Thaw at room temperature for 4 to 5 hours.) Makes 3½ dozen bars.

Apple Meringue Squares

Initial preparation: *About 1¼ hours*
Storage time: *2 days*
Final preparation: *None*

Per serving: 317 calories, 4 g protein, 44 g carbohydrates, 14 g total fat, 88 mg cholesterol, 133 mg sodium

If you're planning an informal dinner later in the week, try this new interpretation of an old-fashioned fruit dessert. It combines buttery shortbread, tart apples, and crisp, light meringue. Store it uncovered to keep the crunchy almond-strewn topping from softening.

- ½ **cup (¼ lb.) butter or margarine**
- 1¼ **cups all-purpose flour**
- 3 **tart green apples (such as Granny Smith)**
- 2 **tablespoons lemon juice**
- 2 **large eggs**
- 1 **cup sugar**
- ¼ **teaspoon baking powder**
- ½ **teaspoon ground cinnamon**
- ½ **cup sliced almonds**

Make-ahead steps: Beat butter and 1 cup of the flour until smooth. Press evenly over bottom of a 7- by 11-inch or 9-inch square baking pan and bake in a 350° oven until golden (about 15 minutes).

Peel, core, and chop apples. Place in a bowl and mix with lemon juice. Arrange evenly over baked crust.

Beat eggs until foamy. Gradually add sugar; continue beating until thick. Mix in baking powder, cinnamon, and remaining ¼ cup flour. Pour evenly over apples; sprinkle almonds on top.

Bake until golden (30 to 35 minutes). Cut into squares and let cool on a rack. Store, uncovered, at room temperature for up to 2 days. Makes 6 to 9 servings.

Crowned with vanilla ice cream, drizzled with thick fudge sauce, and
sprinkled with walnuts, the Ultimate Brownie Sundae (recipe on facing page)
is chewy-gooey devastation to any dieter's will power.

Ginger Shortbread Wedges

Initial preparation: About 1½ hours
Storage time: 5 days at room temperature; 10 months in freezer
Final preparation: None

Per cooky: 211 calories, 2 g protein, 25 g carbohydrates, 12 g total fat, 31 mg cholesterol, 122 mg sodium

Classic shortbread combines just three simple ingredients—butter, sugar, and flour. Ginger introduces an aromatic spiciness that transports the cooky out of the ordinary.

- **2 cups all-purpose flour**
- **1 cup firmly packed brown sugar**
- **1 tablespoon ground ginger**
- **1 cup (½ lb.) butter or margarine, cut into chunks**

Make-ahead steps: In a food processor or bowl, mix flour, sugar, and ginger. Add butter. Whirl or rub with your fingers until mixture resembles coarse cornmeal. Press mixture together to form a large ball.

Press dough evenly over bottom of a 9- or 10-inch round baking pan (with a removable bottom, if possible). Press tines of a fork around edge to form a decorative border; then prick entire surface.

Bake in a 325° oven until golden brown (about 1 hour). Remove from oven and cut into 12 to 16 wedges. Let cool on rack. Run a knife around edge of pan and remove pan rim, or invert pan to remove cookies. Wrap airtight and store at room temperature for up to 5 days. (Or freeze for up to 10 months. Thaw at room temperature for 4 to 5 hours.) Makes 12 to 16 cookies.

Dark Chocolate Chewy Brownies

Initial preparation: About 35 minutes, plus about 1 hour for frosting to cool
Storage time: 2 days at room temperature; 6 months in freezer
Final preparation: None

Per serving: 419 calories, 4 g protein, 49 g carbohydrates, 26 g total fat, 98 mg cholesterol, 124 mg sodium

One bite of our rich, moist brownie will turn you into a chocolate fanatic, if you aren't one already. Add the accompanying dark, semisweet fudge sauce as frosting or warm topping: either way treats you to chocolate perfection.

- **Fudge Sauce (recipe follows)**
- **½ cup (¼ lb.) butter or margarine, cut into chunks**
- **3 ounces unsweetened chocolate**
- **1⅓ cups sugar**
- **2 large eggs**
- **1 teaspoon vanilla**
- **½ cup all-purpose flour**
- **½ cup chopped walnuts or almonds (optional)**

Make-ahead steps: Prepare Fudge Sauce.

In a 2- to 3-quart pan, melt butter and chocolate over low heat, stirring occasionally. Remove from heat; add sugar, eggs, and vanilla; mix well. Add flour and stir until well blended.

Pour into a buttered 8-inch square or round baking pan and spread evenly; sprinkle with nuts, if desired. Bake in a 350° oven until brownie feels firm at edges and springs back in center when gently pressed (about 25 minutes). Let cool on a rack. To frost, pour sauce over brownie and spread evenly. Cover and store at room temperature for up to 2 days. (Or freeze for up to 6 months. Thaw at room temperature for 4 to 5 hours.) Makes 6 to 9 servings.

Fudge Sauce. In a 1- to 2-quart pan, combine ⅓ cup **whipping cream** and 1 cup (6 oz.) **semisweet chocolate chips** or chopped semisweet chocolate. Cook over low heat, stirring, until chocolate is melted. Stir in 1 teaspoon **vanilla** or 2 tablespoons mint-flavored liqueur or rum. Let sauce cool until thick enough to spread (about 1 hour). Or use warm as a sauce. Makes about ¾ cup.

Pictured on facing page

Ultimate Brownie Sundae

Prepare **Dark Chocolate Chewy Brownies,** as directed, but do not frost; cut into 6 equal pieces. Just before serving, prepare **Fudge Sauce.** Set each piece on a dessert plate and top with a ½-cup scoop **vanilla ice cream.** Ladle sauce over ice cream. Garnish with chopped **walnuts** or almonds, if desired. Makes 6 servings.

Brandied Toffee Lace

Initial preparation: About 1¼ hours
Storage time: 2 days in refrigerator; 4 months in freezer
Final preparation: None

Per cooky: 118 calories, 1 g protein, 12 g carbohydrates, 8 g total fat, 14 mg cholesterol, 42 mg sodium

When you're expecting special guests, take time in advance to make these delicate cookies. Each is a sandwich of edible lace enclosing a brandy-flavored chocolate filling, exquisite to eat on its own or with ice cream.

½ cup (¼ lb.) butter or margarine
1 cup quick-cooking rolled oats
½ cup firmly packed brown sugar
⅓ cup all-purpose flour
5 tablespoons whipping cream
1 cup (6 oz.) semisweet chocolate chips
2 tablespoons brandy

Make-ahead steps: In a 1- to 1½-quart pan, melt butter over medium heat. Remove from heat and add oats, sugar, flour, and 2 tablespoons of the cream, stirring until well mixed. For each cooky, drop a teaspoon of the batter on a greased 12- by 15-inch baking sheet, spacing cookies well apart (place only 6 cookies on a sheet). Bake in a 350° oven until lightly browned (7 to 9 minutes).

Let stand until cookies are firm (about 3 minutes). With tip of a pointed knife, ease each cooky free; then lift onto racks to cool.

In a small pan, combine remaining 3 tablespoons cream, chocolate, and brandy. Cook, stir-ring, over lowest heat just until chocolate is melted. Chill until mixture is slightly thickened (10 to 12 minutes). With a small knife or spatula, gently spread a cooky with chocolate mixture and top with a second cooky. Repeat with remaining cookies and chocolate. Wrap airtight and refrigerate for up to 2 days. (Or freeze for up to 4 months. Thaw overnight in refrigerator). Makes about 2 dozen cookies.

Cinnamon-spiced Buñuelos

Initial preparation: About 1½ hours, plus about 20 minutes for dough to rest
Storage time: 1 day
Final preparation: None

Per serving: 189 calories, 2 g protein, 31 g carbohydrates, 7 g total fat, 3 mg cholesterol, .54 mg sodium

So appetizing are these puffs of tender, deep-fried dough that many cuisines include them as desserts.

¼ cup lard or shortening
2 cups all-purpose flour
½ cup lukewarm water
1½ cups sugar
1½ teaspoons ground cinnamon Salad oil

Make-ahead steps: Using 2 knives or a pastry blender, cut lard into flour until fine crumbs form. Sprinkle with water and stir with a fork until dough forms a ball. Knead on a lightly floured board until smooth. Cover and let rest for about 20 minutes.

Divide dough into 12 pieces; shape each into a ball. Keep dough covered with plastic wrap as you work. On a lightly floured board, roll each ball into a 7-inch circle. Stack rounds, separating with wax paper. Combine sugar and cinnamon; set aside.

Pour oil to a depth of 1½ inches into a deep 2- to 3-quart pan or wok and heat to 375°F on a deep-frying thermometer. When oil is hot, cut each dough circle into quarters and slip, one at a time, into oil, without crowding. Cook, turning occasionally, until golden brown (about 1½ minutes). Lift from oil, draining briefly; then dust with sugar-cinnamon mixture. Let cool; wrap airtight and store at room temperature for up to 1 day. Makes 12 to 16 servings.

Fresh Peach Kuchen

Initial preparation: About 50 minutes
Storage time: 2 days
Final preparation: None

Per serving: 309 calories, 5 g protein, 42 g carbohydrates, 14 g total fat, 120 mg cholesterol, 135 mg sodium

Celebrate summer's bounty of fresh, sweet peaches with cinnamon-scented fruit cradled in rich custard on a delicate crust. Cut the creamy kuchen in generous portions, serve, and enjoy.

- ¼ **cup butter or margarine**
- ¼ **teaspoon baking powder**
- 1 **cup all-purpose flour**
- ½ **cup firmly packed brown sugar**
- 2 **large eggs**
- 3 **medium-size peaches, peeled, pitted, and sliced**
- 1 **tablespoon lemon juice**
- ½ **teaspoon ground cinnamon**
- ½ **cup sour cream**

Make-ahead steps: In a bowl, combine butter, baking powder, flour, and 1 tablespoon of the sugar. Rub with your fingers until fine crumbs form. In a small bowl, lightly beat 1 of the eggs. Add 1½ tablespoons of the egg to flour mixture; stir with a fork until evenly distributed. Set aside remaining egg. Press dough evenly over bottom of a 10-inch quiche or pie pan.

Mix peaches with lemon juice; arrange evenly over dough. Mix cinnamon and all but 1 tablespoon of the remaining sugar; sprinkle over peaches. Bake on bottom rack of a 375° oven for 15 minutes.

Meanwhile, in a bowl, combine sour cream, remaining 1 tablespoon sugar, and remaining eggs; beat until blended. Pour over peaches and continue baking until custard jiggles only slightly in center when gently shaken (about 20 minutes). Let cool on a rack; cover and refrigerate for up to 2 days. Makes 6 servings.

Spiced Almond Tart

Initial preparation: About 1¼ hours
Storage time: 2 days at room temperature; 3 months in freezer
Final preparation: None

Per serving: 629 calories, 11 g protein, 54 g carbohydrates, 44 g total fat, 134 mg cholesterol, 157 mg sodium

Cardamom and coriander combine in the creamy almond filling of this mouth-watering tart, enveloped in a rich butter crust.

- **Press-in Pastry (recipe follows)**
- 1¼ **cups *each* whipping cream and sugar**
- ¼ **teaspoon *each* ground cardamom and ground coriander**
- 2 **cups (about 11 oz.) whole blanched almonds**
- ¼ **teaspoon almond extract**

Make-ahead steps: Prepare Press-in Pastry.

In a 2- to 3-quart pan, combine cream, sugar, cardamom, and coriander; bring to a boil over high heat. Reduce heat to medium and simmer, uncovered, stirring often, for 5 minutes. Remove from heat and stir in almonds and almond extract. At once, pour into pastry.

Bake in a 375° oven until golden brown (about 50 minutes). Let stand on a rack until just warm to touch. Remove pan rim and slide a long, slender spatula between crust and pan bottom to free pastry from pan. Let cool; wrap airtight and store at room temperature for up to 2 days. (Or freeze for up to 3 months. Thaw at room temperature for 4 to 5 hours.) Makes 6 to 9 servings.

Press-in Pastry. In a food processor or bowl, combine 1½ cups **all-purpose flour,** 2 tablespoons **sugar,** and ⅔ cup (⅓ lb.) **butter** or margarine, cut into chunks. Whirl or rub with your fingers until fine crumbs form. Add 2 **egg yolks;** whirl or stir with a fork until dough holds together.

Press dough evenly over bottom and up sides of a 10- to 11-inch fluted tart pan with a removable bottom. Bake in a 325° oven until pale golden (about 10 minutes).

Triple Strawberry Pie

Initial preparation: *About 35 minutes, plus about 25 minutes for chilling*
Storage time: *Crust: 1 day; pie: 1 day*
Final preparation: *Garnish*

Per serving: 345 calories, 8 g protein, 39 g carbohydrates, 18 g total fat, 49 mg cholesterol, 312 mg sodium

For strawberry fanciers, this luscious refrigerator pie presents the sweet summer fruit in a crunchy, graham cracker crust. Busy cooks will appreciate preparing this dessert in two easy stages well ahead of serving.

    Honey-Graham Crust (recipe follows)
1½ **envelopes unflavored gelatin**
¼ **cup water**
4 **cups strawberries, washed and hulled**
1 **large package (8 oz.) cream cheese, at room temperature**
2 **tablespoons sugar**
2 **cups strawberry-flavored yogurt**

Make-ahead steps: Prepare Honey-Graham Crust.

In a 1- to 1½-quart pan, sprinkle gelatin over water and let stand until softened (about 5 minutes). Place over low heat and stir until gelatin is dissolved; set aside.

Slice enough strawberries to make 1 cup; set aside. In a blender or food processor, purée enough of the remaining berries to make 1 cup. Set aside remaining whole berries.

In large bowl of an electric mixer, beat cream cheese and sugar until smooth; then beat in yogurt, puréed berries, and gelatin mixture. Stir in sliced strawberries. Cover and chill until mixture begins to set (about 25 minutes).

Spoon into crust. Cover and refrigerate for up to 1 day. Garnish with remaining strawberries. Makes 6 to 8 servings.

Honey-Graham Crust. In a 10-inch pie pan, combine 1½ cups **graham cracker crumbs**, ¼ cup melted **butter** or margarine, and 1 tablespoon **honey;** mix well. Press mixture evenly over bottom and up sides of pan. Bake in a 325° oven until crust smells toasted (about 8 minutes). Let cool; cover and store at room temperature for up to 1 day.

Pumpkin Cheesecake Tart

Initial preparation: *1¼ to 1½ hours, plus at least 1 hour for chilling*
Storage time: *1 day in refrigerator; 4 months in freezer*
Final preparation: *Garnish*

Per serving: 358 calories, 7 g protein, 30 g carbohydrates, 25 g total fat, 113 mg cholesterol, 172 mg sodium

For a Thanksgiving dinner with a difference, serve pumpkin in a creamy cheesecake tart.

    Oat Crust (recipe follows)
1 **large package (8 oz.) and 1 small package (3 oz.) cream cheese, cut into small pieces**
1 **can (16 oz.) pumpkin**
3 **large eggs**
⅔ **cup sugar**
1½ **teaspoons ground cinnamon**
1 **teaspoon** *each* **ground ginger and vanilla**
3 **tablespoons chopped candied ginger (optional)**

Make-ahead steps: Prepare Oat Crust. Meanwhile, in a food processor or blender, whirl cream cheese, pumpkin, eggs, sugar, cinnamon, ground ginger, and vanilla until smooth.

Pour filling into crust. Bake in a 350° oven until filling is set in center when pan is gently shaken (20 to 25 minutes for a 12-inch pan, 30 to 35 minutes for a 9-inch pan). Let cool on a rack; cover and refrigerate for at least 1 hour or for up to 1 day. (Or freeze for up to 4 months. Thaw overnight in refrigerator; or defrost in a microwave following manufacturer's directions.)

To serve: Remove pan rim and garnish with candied ginger, if desired. Makes 12 servings.

Oat Crust. If using a blender, whirl 1 cup **walnuts** until finely ground; place in a bowl. Whirl 1 cup **sweetened shredded coconut** and 1 cup **regular** or quick-cooking **oats** until finely chopped; add to nuts. With your hands, mix in ⅓ cup **sugar** and 6 tablespoons **butter** or margarine, cut into small pieces, until dough holds together. (If using a food processor, whirl nuts, coconut, oats, sugar, and butter until dough holds together.)

Press evenly over bottom and up sides of a 12-inch tart pan with a removable bottom or over bottom and 1 inch up sides of a 9-inch spring-form pan. Bake in a 300° oven until crust feels firm and is lightly browned (35 to 40 minutes). Use immediately.

Strawberries times three—whole, puréed, and flavoring yogurt—fill a sweet
honey-graham crust in Triple Strawberry Pie (recipe on facing page), a cool and
convenient summer treat.

Pictured on page 7

Brazilian Coconut Custard

Initial preparation: *About 1 hour*
Storage time: *2 days*
Final preparation: *About 5 minutes*

Per serving: 251 calories, 3 g protein, 38 g carbohydrates, 10 g total fat, 243 mg cholesterol, 67 mg sodium

Good news for a busy summer social calendar, this cool coconut-flavored custard waits as long as 2 days before you serve it.

> **2 large eggs**
> **10 egg yolks**
> **2 cups sugar**
> **1½ cups cold water**
> **¼ cup butter or margarine, cut in half**
> **1¼ cups sweetened shredded coconut**
> **1 small pineapple (about 3 lbs.)**

Make-ahead steps: In a blender or food processor, combine eggs, egg yolks, sugar, water, and butter; whirl until well blended. Add coconut; whirl just to mix.

Place a 5- to 6-cup ring mold in a larger rimmed baking pan at least 2 inches deep. Pour egg mixture into ring mold. Place both pans in a 350° oven. Fill bottom pan with boiling water halfway up sides of mold. Bake until custard jiggles only slightly when gently shaken (about 50 minutes).

Lift mold from water and place on a rack; let cool completely. Lay a plate on top of mold; hold plate and mold together and invert. Lift off mold; cover and refrigerate for up to 2 days.

To serve: Cut into wedges. Core and peel pineapple; cut into wedges and offer with custard. Makes 12 to 14 servings.

Chocolate-Hazelnut Cheesecake

Initial preparation: *About 1 hour; plus at least 1 hour for chilling*
Storage time: *1 week in refrigerator; 1 month in freezer*
Final preparation: *About 5 minutes*

Per serving: 464 calories, 9 g protein, 29 g carbohydrates, 37 g total fat, 112 mg cholesterol, 189 mg sodium

Italy's candy of hazelnuts and milk chocolate is named *gianduia*. You can make your own mixture, or you can find gianduia in bulk or as candy bars in candy shops.

> **1 large package (8 oz.) and 1 small package (3 oz.) cream cheese, cut into small pieces**
> **¼ cup sugar**
> **1 egg**
> **1½ tablespoons whipping cream**
> **Roasted Hazelnuts with Chocolate (recipe follows) or 8 ounces milk chocolate with hazelnuts (gianduia)**
> **1½ tablespoons hazelnut liqueur**
> **Powdered sugar**
> **Whipped cream**

Make-ahead steps: In large bowl of an electric mixer, beat cream cheese and sugar until well mixed. Add egg and cream and beat until smoothly blended.

Prepare Roasted Hazelnuts with Chocolate. Place in top of a double boiler; set over hot water until melted. Stir chocolate mixture and liqueur into cream cheese mixture.

Butter a 6-inch round baking pan. If pan bottom is not removable, line with wax paper; butter wax paper. If pan bottom can be removed, set pan on a large sheet of foil and fold edges of foil up and slightly above rim to protect pan from seepage. Pour batter into pan.

Set pan in a slightly larger pan and place in middle of a 350° oven. Add boiling water to larger pan until it's about two-thirds up sides of cake pan. Bake until cake is set in center when pan is gently shaken (about 50 minutes). Lift pan from water and let cool on a rack; cover and refrigerate for at least 1 hour or for up to 1 week. (Or freeze for up to 1 month. Thaw overnight in refrigerator; or defrost in a microwave following manufacturer's directions.)

To serve: Run a knife around edge of pan. If pan has a removable bottom, remove rim and set cake on a serving plate. If not, cover top with wax paper. Lay a plate on paper; hold pan and plate together and quickly flip. Lift off pan and peel off paper lining. Lay a small serving plate on cake; holding plates together, quickly flip. Dust cake lightly with powdered sugar. Accompany with whipped cream. Makes 6 servings.

Roasted Hazelnuts with Chocolate. Spread ⅔ cup (3 oz.) **hazelnuts** in an 8- or 9-inch baking pan. Bake in an 350° oven until nuts are golden under skin (8 to 10 minutes). Let cool. Rub in a towel to remove as much brown skin as possible. Discard skins. In a food processor or blender, whirl nuts into a paste. Combine with 5 ounces chopped **milk chocolate.**

White Chocolate Fruit Terrine

Initial preparation: About 45 minutes, plus at least 3 hours for chilling
Storage time: 1 week in refrigerator; 4 months in freezer
Final preparation: About 5 minutes

Per serving: 275 calories, 3 g protein, 22 g carbohydrates, 20 g total fat, 28 mg cholesterol, 24 mg sodium

When you've had a hectic week and company's coming any minute, you'll be glad to have this magnificent dessert tucked in the refrigerator. Present thin slices with whipped cream.

Chopped Toasted Hazelnuts (recipe follows)

10 ounces **finely chopped white chocolate or white chocolate chips**

1½ cups **whipping cream**

¼ teaspoon **vanilla**

6 tablespoons **port**

¾ cup **chopped dried or glazed apricots**

½ cup **chopped dates**

2 or 3 **whole hazelnuts**
Several slivers dried or glazed apricots

Make-Ahead Steps: Prepare Chopped Toasted Hazelnuts; set aside.

Place chocolate in a bowl. Set over a pan of hot water (water should not touch bowl). In a 1- to 2-quart pan, bring ½ cup of the cream to a boil over medium-high heat. Add to chocolate; stir until smooth. Stir in vanilla and 3 tablespoons of the port. Reserving ½ cup of the chopped hazelnuts, stir in remaining chopped nuts, apricots, and dates.

Evenly spread ¼ cup of the reserved chopped nuts in a 3- to 4-cup straight-sided mold. Spoon chocolate mixture into mold, pushing down and smoothing surface. Sprinkle remaining ¼ cup chopped nuts on top and press lightly into chocolate. Cover and refrigerate for at least 3 hours or for up to 1 week. (Or freeze for up to 4 months. Thaw overnight in refrigerator; or defrost in a microwave following manufacturer's directions.)

To serve: Unmold by dipping mold to just below rim in hottest tap water for about 30 seconds. Invert onto a flat serving dish and tap to release terrine. Garnish with hazelnuts and apricot slivers.

In a bowl, combine remaining 1 cup cream and remaining 3 tablespoons port; beat until cream holds very soft peaks. Offer with terrine. Makes 12 to 16 servings.

Chopped Toasted Hazelnuts. Spread 1¾ cups **hazelnuts** in an 8- or 9-inch baking pan and bake in a 350° oven until nuts are golden under skin (about 20 minutes). Let cool. Rub in a towel to remove as much brown skin as possible. Finely chop nuts.

Chestnut Truffle Torte

Initial preparation: About 2½ hours, plus at least 2 hours for chilling
Storage time: 5 days
Final preparation: None

Per serving: 601 calories, 8 g protein, 79 g carbohydrates, 32 g total fat, 149 mg cholesterol, 42 mg sodium

When you're feeling wicked early in the week, whip up this extravaganza of chocolate, chestnuts, brandy, and cream. It keeps for several days without losing a single calorie.

¼ cup **unsalted butter or margarine**

⅔ cup **sugar**

5 **large eggs, separated**

2 cans (8¾ oz. *each*) **chestnut spread**

½ cup **all-purpose flour**

¼ cup *each* **brandy and whipping cream or ½ cup whipping cream**

1 pound **semisweet chocolate, melted and cooled**
Chocolate Icing (recipe follows)

Make-ahead steps: In a bowl, combine butter, sugar, and egg yolks; beat until fluffy. Beat in chestnut spread, flour, brandy, cream, and chocolate.

In another bowl, beat egg whites until moist, stiff peaks form. Gently fold into butter mixture; pour into a buttered 9-inch spring-form pan. Bake in a 325° oven until firm in center when lightly pressed (about 1¼ hours).

Meanwhile, prepare Chocolate Icing. Let torte cool on a rack for 10 minutes. Run a knife around edge of pan; remove pan rim. Let cool; then frost. Cover and refrigerate for at least 2 hours or for up to 5 days. Makes 10 to 12 servings.

Chocolate Icing. In a 1- to 1½-quart pan, combine ¾ cup **whipping cream,** 1 tablespoon **unsalted butter** or margarine, and 4 ounces **semisweet chocolate.** Cook, stirring, over low heat just until chocolate is melted. Chill until thick (about 1 hour).

Decoratively molded Lemon-glazed Butter Cake (recipe on facing page) slices
into rich, moist refreshment. Its citrus garnish echoes the cake's glazing of
sweet-tart lemon syrup.

French Almond Cake

Initial preparation: About 1 hour
Storage time: 1 day at room temperature; 2 months in freezer
Final preparation: Garnish (optional)

Per serving: 183 calories, 4 g protein, 26 g carbohydrates, 7 g total fat, 114 mg cholesterol, 73 mg sodium

Choose either marzipan or almond paste to flavor this elegant cake. Marzipan, with fewer almonds and more sugar, results in a cake with a finer and lighter texture.

- **7 to 8 ounces (about ¾ cup) marzipan or almond paste**
- **3 large eggs**
- **2 teaspoons kirsch, orange-flavored liqueur, or vanilla**
- **2 tablespoons *each* all-purpose flour and cornstarch**
- **3 tablespoons butter or margarine, melted and cooled**
  Powdered sugar (optional)

Make-ahead steps: Crumble marzipan into large bowl of an electric mixer. Add eggs, one at a time, beating well each addition. Beat on high speed until thick, light, and doubled in volume (about 15 minutes). Beat in kirsch. Sift flour and cornstarch over batter; gently fold in. Pour in melted butter; fold in gently until blended. Pour into a buttered 8-inch round cake pan.

Bake in a 325° oven until cake begins to pull away from pan sides and feels set when lightly touched in center (30 to 35 minutes). Let cool in pan on a rack for 10 minutes. Invert from pan onto rack and let cool; cover and store at room temperature for up to 1 day. (Or freeze for up to 2 months. Thaw at room temperature for 4 to 5 hours.)

To serve: If desired, sift sugar over top. Makes 6 to 8 servings.

Pictured on facing page

Lemon-glazed Butter Cake

Initial preparation: About 1½ hours, plus at least 6 hours for cooling
Storage time: 1 day at room temperature; 4 months in freezer
Final preparation: Garnish

Per serving: 512 calories, 6 g protein, 84 g carbohydrates, 18 g total fat, 113 mg cholesterol, 259 mg sodium

Lemons give refreshing tang to this handsome cake. The aromatic peel goes into the batter; the tart juice, combined with powdered sugar, becomes a thin glaze that soaks into the baked cake, adding moistness and refreshing flavor.

- **1 cup (½ lb.) butter or margarine, at room temperature**
- **1¼ cups sugar**
- **3 large eggs**
- **2 teaspoons *each* baking powder and grated lemon peel**
- **¾ teaspoon almond extract**
- **3 cups all-purpose flour**
- **1 cup milk**
  Lemon Glaze (recipe follows)
  Lemon slices
  Citrus leaves, washed and dried

Make-ahead steps: In large bowl of an electric mixer, combine butter and sugar; beat on high speed until fluffy (about 5 minutes). Beat in eggs, one at a time; then mix in baking powder, lemon peel, and almond extract. Add flour and milk alternately, beating well on low speed after each addition.

Pour batter into a well-buttered and flour-dusted 9- or 10-cup plain or decorative tube pan. Tap pan on counter several times to level batter and eliminate any air pockets. Bake in center of a 325° oven until cake begins to pull away from pan sides (about 1 hour). Meanwhile, prepare Lemon Glaze; set aside.

Set pan on a rack and let stand for 5 minutes. Run a sharp knife around edge of tube to loosen cake. Place rack on top of pan and invert gently to release cake. Invert again to return cake to pan.

With a thin wooden skewer, pierce cake at 1-inch intervals. Pour all but ½ cup of the glaze over hot cake. Let cool completely (at least 6 hours); then invert cake onto a serving plate and remove pan. Stir reserved glaze and spoon evenly over top. Cover and store at room temperature for up to 1 day. (Or freeze for up to 4 months. Thaw at room temperature overnight.)

To serve: Garnish with lemon slices and leaves. Makes 10 to 12 servings.

Lemon Glaze. Smoothly blend ¾ cup **lemon juice** into 3½ cups (1 lb.) unsifted **powdered sugar.**

Parties with a Punch

Entertaining at your next big event will be all the easier if you prepare drinks a day in advance. Begin with a mixture of fruit juice or egg and cream, and store until serving time. Then just add fruit, wine, whipped cream, or sparkling water—and celebrate.

Praline Eggnog

- 1¼ cups sugar
- 3 to 6 cups milk
- 3 cinnamon sticks (*each* about 3 inches long)
- 1 vanilla bean (about 7 inches long), cut in half lengthwise
- 2 cups whipping cream
- 12 large eggs
  Freshly grated or ground nutmeg

Make-ahead steps: In a 3- to 4-quart pan, melt half the sugar over high heat. Shake pan frequently as sugar begins to melt, then tilt pan constantly to keep liquid well mixed until it turns pale amber. Watch closely to prevent scorching. Remove from heat; at once add 3 cups of the milk, cinnamon sticks, and vanilla bean (mixture will sputter).

Return pan to medium heat and stir until caramelized sugar is dissolved. Cover and refrigerate for at least 3 hours or for up to 1 day. Remove cinnamon sticks and vanilla bean.

Whip 1 cup of the cream; set aside. Whip eggs with remaining sugar until about tripled in volume; then whisk egg mixture and cream into milk mixture. For a less rich eggnog, add as much of the remaining 3 cups milk as desired. Cover and refrigerate for up to 2 days.

To serve: Whip remaining 1 cup cream until it holds soft peaks. Whisk eggnog gently to blend, then top with whipped cream and nutmeg. Dip down into punch as you serve. Makes 16 to 20 servings.

Per serving: 189 calories, 5 g protein, 16 g carbohydrates, 12 g total fat, 196 mg cholesterol, 68 mg sodium

Sangria

- 5 cups dry red wine
- 1 cup orange juice
- ½ cup lemon juice
- 2 cups sparkling water
- 1 lemon, thinly sliced

Make-ahead steps: In a large bowl, mix wine, orange juice, and lemon juice. Cover and refrigerate for up to 1 day.

To serve: Pour into a small punch bowl. Add sparkling water and lemon slices. Makes about 10 servings (about 2 quarts).

Per serving: 101 calories, .55 g protein, 7 g carbohydrates, .07 g total fat, 0 mg cholesterol, 9 mg sodium

Mulled Apple-Ginger Sparkler

- 2 cups apple juice
- ½ cup preserved ginger in syrup, chopped
- 8 cinnamon sticks (*each* about 3 inches long)
- 2 bottles (750 ml. *each*) cold brut-style dry sparkling wine

Make-ahead steps: In a 1- to 2-quart pan, combine apple juice, ginger with syrup, and cinnamon. Bring to a boil over high heat.

Cook, uncovered, stirring occasionally, until juice is reduced to 1 cup (about 30 minutes). Let cool; cover and refrigerate for up to 1 day.

To serve: For each serving, spoon about 2 tablespoons apple-ginger syrup and 1 cinnamon stick into a glass (6- to 8-oz. size). Fill glass with wine. Makes about 8 servings.

Per serving: 149 calories, .25 g protein, 15 g carbohydrates, .09 g total fat, 0 mg cholesterol, 14 mg sodium

Holiday Punch

- 1 cup *each* sugar and water
- 2 cups grapefruit juice
- ½ cup *each* lemon juice, lime juice, and orange juice
- 2 cups chilled club soda
- 1½ quarts dry to moderately sweet white wine (such as Chenin Blanc)
- 1 *each* orange, lemon, and lime, thinly sliced
  Ice cubes

Make-ahead steps: In a 1- to 2-quart pan, combine sugar and water. Bring to a boil over medium-high heat, stirring until sugar is dissolved; let cool. Add grapefruit juice, lemon juice, lime juice, and orange juice. Cover and refrigerate for up to 1 day.

To serve: Pour juice mixture into a 5- to 6-quart punch bowl. Pour in club soda and wine; add orange, lemon, and lime slices, and ice. Makes about 16 servings (about 3 quarts).

Per serving: 127 calories, .33 g protein, 18 g carbohydrates, .06 g total fat, 0 mg cholesterol, 14 mg sodium

Melon-Mint Sorbet

Initial preparation: About 30 minutes, plus about 1 hour for chilling and at least 4 hours for freezing
Storage time: 1 month
Final preparation: None

Per serving: 77 calories, .47 g protein, 20 g carbohydrates, .10 g total fat, 0 mg cholesterol, 11 mg sodium

Our herbed fruit sorbet brings any meal to a fresh and cool conclusion. Easy to make when melons reach their peak of sweetness, the dessert waits conveniently in the freezer for up to a month.

⅓ cup *each* water and sugar

1 medium-size honeydew melon (about 2¾ lbs.) or 3 small cantaloupes (about 4½ lbs. *total*), cut in half and seeded

2 tablespoons *each* lemon juice and finely chopped mint leaves

Make-ahead steps: In a 1- to 2-quart pan, bring water and sugar to a boil over high heat; stir until sugar is dissolved. Chill until cool (about 1 hour).

Meanwhile, scoop melon from rind. Whirl in a food processor or blender until puréed; you should have about 3 cups.

Add purée, lemon juice, and mint to syrup. Pour sorbet mixture into a 9- by 13-inch pan; cover and freeze for about 2 hours.

Break into small chunks; and whirl in a food processor or beat with an electric mixer until smooth. Place in an airtight container and freeze for at least 2 hours or for up to 1 month. Makes 4 to 6 servings.

Chilled Zabaglione with Fruit

Initial preparation: About 30 minutes, plus at least 1 hour for chilling
Storage time: 1 day
Final preparation: About 10 minutes

Per serving: 256 calories, 4 g protein, 23 g carbohydrates, 15 g total fat, 243 mg cholesterol, 31 mg sodium

Classic zabaglione, Italy's frothy egg pudding, must be prepared and served at once. In this variation, though, the velvety dessert can be made the day before. The egg yolks, sugar, and wine are cooked in the traditional manner, then folded with vanilla ice cream and whipped cream.

¾ cup vanilla ice cream

6 egg yolks

⅓ cup sugar

¼ cup dry or sweet white wine

¼ cup dry or sweet Marsala

1 cup whipping cream

2 to 3 tablespoons orange-flavored liqueur

3 to 4 cups *total* peeled and sliced kiwi fruit, sliced strawberries, fresh pineapple chunks, or fresh orange segments (or some of each)

Make-ahead steps: Spoon ice cream into a bowl and let stand until soft.

Meanwhile, in a round-bottomed zabaglione pan or in top of a double boiler, mix egg yolks, sugar, white wine, and Marsala. Place round-bottomed pan over medium-low heat or bring water in bottom of double boiler to a simmer. Cook, whipping rapidly with a wire whisk or electric mixer, until mixture is tripled in volume and flows in thick ribbons from beater (about 5 minutes).

Remove pan from heat and stir zabaglione for a few seconds; then add to ice cream and mix well. Let cool to room temperature (about 15 minutes).

Meanwhile, beat cream until it holds soft peaks; fold into ice cream mixture. Stir in liqueur to taste. Cover and refrigerate for at least 1 hour or for up to 1 day.

To serve: Spoon fruit equally into stemmed glasses and add zabaglione. Makes 6 to 8 servings.

Index

This Armenian sandwich, filled with spicy ground lamb, is called
Lahmejun (recipe on page 37). Our version is served on flour tortillas with
cucumbers, tomatoes, chiles, and feta cheese.